Anthony

 W9-AVC-912

TREASURY OF LITERATURE

INTEGRATED SPELLING

GRADE 2

HARCOURT BRACE & COMPANY

Orlando Atlanta Austin Boston San Francisco Chicago Dallas New York
Toronto London

Copyright © by Harcourt Brace & Company

All rights reserved. No part of this publication may be reproduced or
transmitted in any form or by any means, electronic or mechanical, including
photocopy, recording, or any information storage and retrieval system.

Permission is granted for the printing of complete pages for instructional
use and not for resale by any teacher using TREASURY OF LITERATURE.

Printed in the United States of America

ISBN 0-15-302069-5

12   082   2000

Contents

MAKING

This book gives you a place to keep a word list of your own. It's called a Spelling Log!

If you need some ideas for making your list, just look at what my friends are doing!

African Springbok

When I read, I look for words I think are interesting.

I listen for new words on radio and TV.

...and now, news about a strange discovery.....

I'll add words that I need to use when I write. Words that are hard for me to spell belong here, too.

canine?

My Pet Canine

Before I put a word in my log, I check the spelling. I look up the word in a dictionary, or I ask a classmate for help.

To help me understand and remember the meaning of a word, I write a definition or draw a picture. I use the word in a sentence, too.

SIDEWALKS SING • Harcourt Brace School Publishers

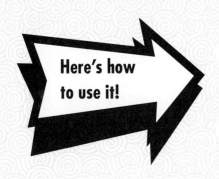

Here's how to use it!

The Spelling Log in this book is just for you. It's your own list of words that you want to remember. Your Spelling Log has three parts. Here's how to use each part.

This handy list makes it easy for me to study the words I need to learn!

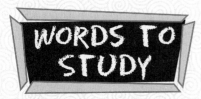

WORDS TO STUDY

This is where you will list the words from each lesson that you need to study. Write the words you miss on the pretest. Add other words that you are not sure you can always spell correctly.

SIDEWALKS SING • Harcourt Brace School Publishers

Hints on the sides of the pages may help you think of ways to group your words.

NOISY WORDS

FANCY WORDS

I'll write a clue with each word to help me remember it.

Have fun!

Words to Explore

These pages are for listing the Words to Explore from each spelling lesson. Place the words in whatever groups you like. Then write them on the pages where you think they belong. You will find pages for language, social studies, math and science, and art and music.

MY OWN WORD COLLECTION

You choose the words to list on these pages. Add new words and other words you want to remember. You choose how to group them, too!

SIDEWALKS SING • Harcourt Brace School Publishers

STUDY STEPS TO LEARN A WORD

Check out these steps.

SAY THE WORD.

REMEMBER WHEN YOU HAVE HEARD THE WORD USED. THINK ABOUT WHAT IT MEANS.

LOOK AT THE WORD.

FIND ANY WORD PARTS YOU KNOW. THINK ABOUT OTHER WORDS THAT HAVE SPELLINGS OR MEANINGS ALMOST LIKE IT. PICTURE THE WORD IN YOUR MIND.

SAY

1

LOOK

2

SIDEWALKS SING • Harcourt Brace School Publishers

SPELL THE WORD TO YOURSELF.

THINK ABOUT THE WAY EACH SOUND IS SPELLED.

WRITE THE WORD WHILE YOU ARE LOOKING AT IT.

CHECK THE WAY YOU HAVE FORMED YOUR LETTERS. IF YOU HAVE NOT WRITTEN THE WORD CLEARLY OR CORRECTLY, WRITE IT AGAIN.

CHECK WHAT YOU LEARNED.

COVER THE WORD AND WRITE IT. IF YOU DID NOT SPELL THE WORD CORRECTLY, PRACTICE THE STUDY STEPS UNTIL YOU CAN WRITE IT CORRECTLY EVERY TIME.

SIDEWALKS SING • Harcourt Brace School Publishers

Integrated Spelling

Words with Short a

Spelling WORDS

1. an
2. bad
3. bat
4. map
5. had
6. dad
7. sat
8. sad
9. cat
10. mad

YOUR OWN WORDS

Look for other words with the short a sound. Write them here.

11. glad
12. flap

Each Spelling Word has the short a sound. Say each word aloud. What other words does it rhyme with?

Write the Spelling Words under rhyming words to help you remember them.

pad
bad
mad
dad
sad
had

rat
cat
bat
mat

tap
nap

pan
an

The short a sound can be spelled a.

SIDEWALKS SING "Ronald Morgan Goes to Bat" • Harcourt Brace School Publishers

Integrated Spelling

Name _____

STRATEGY Workshop

SPELLING CLUES: Rhyming Words Think about rhyming words. How do you spell them? Try those spellings. Does the word look right?

Circle the words in each group that rhyme. Then write the rhyming words.

1. Hi. My name is (Tad.)
   Which words rhyme
   with my name?

   mad _mad_

   man _____

   had _had_

   bad _bad_

2. Hi. My name is (Pat.)
   Which words rhyme
   with my name?

   bat _bat_

   ban _____

   sat _sat_

   had _____

Write a Spelling Word that rhymes with the underlined word.

A _map_ is on his <u>lap</u>.

Her _dad_ has a <u>pad</u>.

This _cat_ likes the <u>bat</u>.

Fun with Words Write a Spelling Word to complete each picture caption.

4. A _bad_ Day

5. _an_ Excellent Day

SIDEWALKS SING "Ronald Morgan Goes to Bat" • Harcourt Brace School Publishers

Name _____

VOCABULARY WordShop

Write a Word to Explore in each shape.

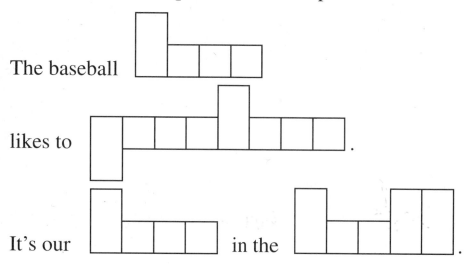

The baseball

likes to _____ .

It's our _____ in the _____ .

Words to Explore
. . . .
field

practice

team

turn

LABEL THE PICTURE Label the clothes you might wear to play baseball. Use the words in the bat.

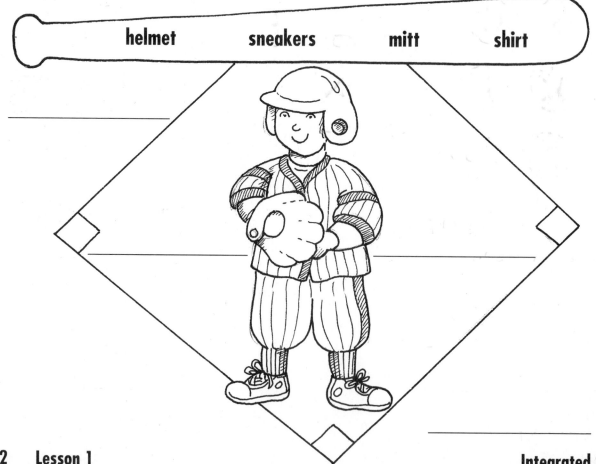

helmet   sneakers   mitt   shirt

SIDEWALKS SING "Ronald Morgan Goes to Bat" • Harcourt Brace School Publishers

Integrated Spelling

Name _____

What's in a Word?

A <u>bat</u> is something you use to play baseball. Can you think of another kind of bat?

Draw a picture for each kind of bat. Label your pictures.

_____   _____

Write another word that can mean different things. _____

TRY THIS Write each group of Spelling Words in ABC order. Look at the first letter of each word to help you.

1. cat _____   2. sat _____

   dad _____   map _____

   bad _____   had _____

   an _____   dad _____

SIDEWALKS SING "Ronald Morgan Goes to Bat" • Harcourt Brace School Publishers

Integrated Spelling

Name Anthony

Words with Short e

Spelling WORDS

1. bet
2. men
3. egg
4. yes
5. ten
6. mess
7. wet
8. leg
9. set
10. yet

YOUR OWN WORDS

Look for other words with the short e sound. Write them here.

11. geco
12. Ed

Each Spelling Word has the short e sound. Say each word aloud. Where do you hear the short e sound?

On the sidewalk, write the words that have the short e sound in the middle. On the sign, write the word that has the short e sound at the beginning.

bet   men
ten   yes
mess   wet
leg   egg
set
yet

The short e sound can be spelled e.

14   Lesson 2

Integrated Spelling

SIDEWALKS SING "Matthew and Tilly" • Harcourt Brace School Publishers

Name Anthony

STRATEGY Workshop

PROOFREADING: Checking Spelling After you write, check your spelling. Circle words you aren't sure of. Then check the spelling.

How do you spell each Spelling Word? Choose the correct spelling and write it.

1. yett   (yet)   _yet_
2. seet   (set)   _set_
3. eg   (egg)   _egg_
4. tenn   (ten)   _ten_

This telephone call has three spelling mistakes. Write the misspelled words correctly.

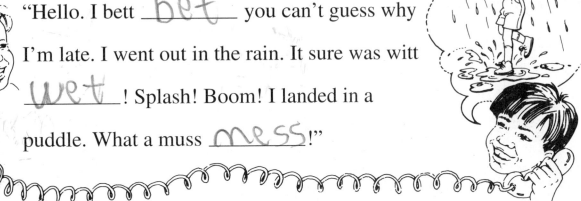

"Hello. I bett _bet_ you can't guess why I'm late. I went out in the rain. It sure was witt _wet_ ! Splash! Boom! I landed in a puddle. What a muss _mess_ !"

Fun with Words Write a Spelling Word to complete the name rhymes.

5. Meg has egg on her _leg_.

6. Ben knows when to call ten _men_.

7. Bess said, "_yes_, I made that mess."

SIDEWALKS SING "Matthew and Tilly" • Harcourt Brace School Publishers

Name _____

VOCABULARY WordShop

Look at the pictures. Write a Word to Explore in each blank of the story.

Words to Explore

began

bike

brave

once

_____ it was raining hard.

My friend fell off her _____.

She was very _____.

I fixed her knee.

We _____ to laugh.

That's what friends are for!

What's in a Word?

Friend comes from a word that means "to love."

Write a sentence. Tell what you love about one of your friends.

_____

_____

SIDEWALKS SING "Matthew and Tilly" • Harcourt Brace School Publishers

Integrated Spelling

SYNONYMS What are some other words that mean almost the same as <u>friend</u>?
Write a synonym for <u>friend</u> under each picture.

_____   _____

CLASSIFYING Who are your friends? What do you do with them? Where do
you go? Complete the chart to show.

Friends	Things You Do	Places You Go
_____	_____	_____
_____	_____	_____
_____	_____	_____

WITH A FRIEND Write a story. Use six Spelling Words in your story. Then
read your story. Circle the Spelling Words. Make sure you spelled them
correctly.

Integrated Spelling

SIDEWALKS SING "Matthew and Tilly" • Harcourt Brace School Publishers

Name Anthony

Words with Short i

SIDEWALKS SING "Arthur's Pet Business" • Harcourt Brace School Publishers

Spelling WORDS

1. pin
2. sit
3. if
4. fix
5. hid
6. him
7. hill
8. six
9. win
10. bit

YOUR OWN WORDS

Look for other words with the short i sound. Write them here.

11. mitten
12. miss

Each Spelling Word has the short i sound. Say each word aloud. Where do you hear the short i sound?

On the bows, write the words with the short i sound in the middle. On the dog's collar, write the word with the short i sound in the beginning.

pin
fix

sit
hid

him
six

hill
win

bit

if

The short i sound can be spelled i.

Integrated Spelling

STRATEGY Workshop

SPELLING CLUES: Rhyming Words Thinking about rhyming words can help you spell new words. Try using spellings you already know.

Find the words in each row that rhyme. Circle the letters that are the same. Then write the rhyming words.

1. win   him   pin   _win_   _pin_
2. one   six   fix   _six_   _fix_
3. bit   bite   sit   _bit_   _sit_

Write the Spelling Words to finish the silly rhymes that tell about the pictures.

4. The kid _hid_.   5. Gill is on the _hil_.   6. A rim for _him_!

Fun with Words Write a Spelling Word to tell about the pictures.

_If_ _____ at first you don't succeed, try, try again.

SIDEWALKS SING "Arthur's Pet Business" • Harcourt Brace School Publishers

Name _____

VOCABULARY WordShop

Use Words to Explore to tell about the calendar.

Words to Explore

dollar

earn

phone

work

	Monday	Tuesday	Wednesday	Thursday	Friday
Week 1	Got pet-sitting job today		Work 1 Hour	Work 2 Hours	Earn $3
Week 2		Work 1 Hour			Earn $1
Week 3				Call for more jobs	

On Wednesday, I will start my _____.

The first week I will _____ 3 dollars.

The second week I will earn 1 _____.

The third week I will call my customers on the _____.

What's in a Word?

Job means work. If you do "odd jobs," you do different kinds of work. If you work "by the job," you get paid for the job you do.

What "odd jobs" would you like to do? How much would you get paid "by the job" for each "odd job" you do? Complete the chart to show.

Odd Jobs

Pay by Job	Walk dog		
	$1.00		

SIDEWALKS SING "Arthur's Pet Business" • Harcourt Brace School Publishers

Integrated Spelling

Name _____

NOUNS Look at the pictures of parents doing jobs.
Label each picture with a word from the box.

mother   father

1. _____   2. _____

SYNONYMS What other words mean the same as <u>mother</u> and <u>father</u>?
Make two lists. Use words from the frame and some of your own.

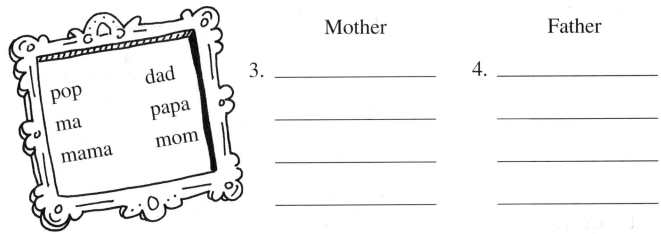

pop   dad
ma   papa
mama   mom

Mother   Father

3. _____   4. _____

_____   _____

_____   _____

_____   _____

WITH A PARTNER Draw pictures for three Spelling Words. Have your partner
draw pictures for three other Spelling Words. Exchange pictures. Label each
other's pictures.

Integrated Spelling

SIDEWALKS SING "Arthur's Pet Business" • Harcourt Brace School Publishers

Name Anthony

Words with Short O

1. top
2. lot
3. mom
4. doll
5. rock
6. box
7. stop
8. pond
9. job
10. fox

Each Spelling Word has the short o sound. Say each word aloud. Where do you hear the short o sound?

Write the words in two groups to help you remember them.

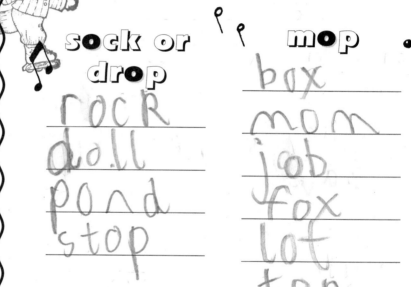

sock or drop

rock
doll
pond
stop

mop

box
mom
job
fox
lot
top

YOUR OWN WORDS

Look for other words with the short o sound. Write them here.

11. cop
12. pop

The short o sound can be spelled o.

SIDEWALKS SING "I Have a Sister—My Sister Is Deaf" • Harcourt Brace School Publishers

Name Anthony

![STRATEGY Workshop]

SPELLING CLUES: Spelling Rules Think about ways to spell short vowel sounds. Write the word. Does it look right?

Which spelling is for a word with a short vowel sound? Write the spelling that is correct.

1. (top)   toop   _top_

2. foax   (fox)   _fox_

3. boex   (box)   _box_

4. (job)   joob   _job_

5. loat   (lot)   _lot_

Write the correct spelling to finish the sentences.

6. The frog jumps in the _pond_ .
   pond   ponde

7. Cars _stop_ at the red light.
   step   (stop)

8. The _doll_ says "Mama."
   dole   (doll)

9. My kitten purrs when I _rock_ it.
   (rock)   rok

Fun with Words Write the Spelling Word that is the same forward and backward. _mom_

SIDEWALKS SING "I Have a Sister—My Sister Is Deaf" • Harcourt Brace School Publishers

Name _____

VOCABULARY WordShop

Use a Word to Explore to complete each sentence.

Words to Explore
· · · · · · · · · · · · ·
listen
sound
touch
gentle

My sister plays music. I showed her how to _____ the keys. The

music isn't _____. It is very loud. My sister can't hear it, but she

can feel the _____. I like to _____ to her music.

What's in a Word?

One kind of special sound is a musical <u>chord</u>. You play a
<u>chord</u> on the piano, but you tie a box with a <u>cord</u>. <u>Chord</u> and
<u>cord</u> sound alike but mean different things.

Write <u>chord</u> or <u>cord</u> to complete each sentence.

I played the _____ on the piano.

I tied a _____ around the box.

Now think of two other words that sound the same but mean different things.
Write a sentence for each one.

1. _____

2. _____

SIDEWALKS SING "I Have a Sister—My Sister Is Deaf" • Harcourt Brace School Publishers

Name _____

SENSE WORDS Write one sense word to tell about each sentence.

| touch | see | taste | hear | smell |

I _____ with my .

I _____ with my .

I _____ with my .

I _____ with my .

I _____ with my .

TRY THIS! Make shapes for five Spelling Words. Then exchange shapes with a friend. Write the Spelling Words that fit the shapes. More than one word might fit!

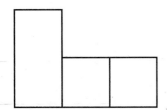 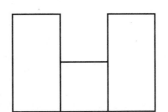 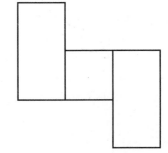

SIDEWALKS SING "I Have a Sister—My Sister Is Deaf" • Harcourt Brace School Publishers

Integrated Spelling

Name _____

Practice Test

A. Read each pair of sentences. Circle the underlined word that is spelled correctly in the sentence.

1. My <u>dad</u> took me to a baseball game.
    My <u>did</u> took me to a baseball game.

2. The <u>mon</u> on the team wore striped pants.
    The <u>men</u> on the team wore striped pants.

3. We hoped our team would <u>wen</u>.
    We hoped our team would <u>win</u>.

4. Being a baseball player is a great <u>jab</u>.
    Being a baseball player is a great <u>job</u>.

5. One player got <u>mad</u> when he struck out.
    One player got <u>med</u> when he struck out.

6. Another player fell and hurt his <u>lag</u>.
    Another player fell and hurt his <u>leg</u>.

7. The best player batted in <u>sox</u> runs.
    The best player batted in <u>six</u> runs.

SIDEWALKS SING Unit 1 Review • Harcourt Brace School Publishers

Integrated Spelling

Name _____

B. Read each pair of sentences. Circle the underlined word that is spelled correctly in the sentence.

1. I love to <u>sit</u> and watch games.
   I love to <u>sot</u> and watch games.

2. It's a <u>lut</u> of fun to keep score.
   It's a <u>lot</u> of fun to keep score.

3. My <u>mom</u> likes the hot dogs and peanuts.
   My <u>mam</u> likes the hot dogs and peanuts.

4. When it rains, everyone gets <u>wit</u>.
   When it rains, everyone gets <u>wet</u>.

5. Sometimes they have to <u>step</u> the game.
   Sometimes they have to <u>stop</u> the game.

6. I feel <u>bad</u> if our team loses.
   I feel <u>bed</u> if our team loses.

7. I always want my team on <u>tip</u>.
   I always want my team on <u>top</u>.

8. I told my dad I <u>had</u> a great time!
   I told my dad I <u>hod</u> a great time!

SIDEWALKS SING Unit 1 Review • Harcourt Brace School Publishers

Name _____

WATCH ME WORK

Think about all the ways you could earn money. Look at the pictures and write a sentence about each one.

_____

_____

_____

Words
to Watch For
....

aunt

bought

people

snow

store

time

_____

_____

_____

_____

_____

_____

TIPS FOR SPELLING SUCCESS Make sure that all your sentences are statements. Check to see that your sentences begin with capital letters and end with periods. Read your sentences one more time and look for spelling errors.

SIDEWALKS SING Unit 1 Review • Harcourt Brace School Publishers

Integrated Spelling

CHILDREN IN BOOKS

Think about the boys and girls you have read about in class. Choose two, and make a list about each child. Write down ideas about the children you chose. What are they like? What are their families like? Who are their friends? Then look at the two lists. How are the two children alike? How are they different? Show your lists to a friend.

TIPS FOR SPELLING SUCCESS Be sure that you started each name with a capital letter. Read your lists again and check your spelling.

WORD DOODLES

Read the clues. Then change the vowel to spell a new word.

man	more than one man	_____
fix	an animal	_____
tap	a spinning toy	_____
did	father	_____

TIPS FOR SPELLING SUCCESS Use what you know about short vowel sounds to help you spell new words.

SIDEWALKS SING Unit 1 Review • Harcourt Brace School Publishers

Name _____

Words with Short u

Spelling WORDS

1. us
2. cup
3. dug
4. much
5. duck
6. mud
7. bus
8. cut
9. must
10. jump

YOUR OWN WORDS

Look for other words with the short u sound. Write them here.

11. _____
12. _____

Each Spelling Word has the short u sound. Say each word aloud. Listen for the short u sound.

Write the Spelling Words in two groups to help you remember them.

luck

much
duck
must
jump

but

us
cup
dug
mud
bus
cut

The short u sound is spelled u.

SIDEWALKS SING "The Wolf's Chicken Stew" • Harcourt Brace School Publishers

Name _____

STRATEGY Workshop

SPELLING CLUES: Sounds and Letters Say the word. Listen for the vowel sound.
Did you spell the sound correctly?

Change the vowel to <u>u</u> in each word.
Write the Spelling Word.

1. cot _cut_

2. is _us_

3. dog _dug_

4. mast _must_

Answer the riddles. Change the vowels to make Spelling Words.

5. I can fly.
   I can swim.
   I am a <u>deck</u>. _duck_

6. I'm dirt when I'm dry.
   When I'm wet, I'm <u>mad</u>. _mud_

7. I hold water.
   You drink from me.
   I'm a <u>cap</u>. _cup_

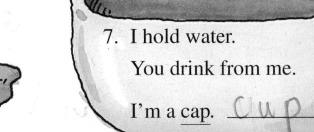

Fun with Words Do the math. Write a Spelling Word.

8. j + u t + m p − t = _jump_

9. a b − a + u s = _bus_

10. s + m u + c − s + h = _much_

SIDEWALKS SING "The Wolf's Chicken Stew" • Harcourt Brace School Publishers

Integrated Spelling

Name _____

VOCABULARY WordShop

What are the animals saying? Use Words
to Explore to complete each sentence.

SIDEWALKS SING "The Wolf's Chicken Stew" • Harcourt Brace School Publishers

Words
to Explore
· · · · · · · · · · · · · ·
delicious
stew
perfect
cookies

Who made these one

hundred _____ _____ ?

This _____

is _____ .

What's in a Word?

<u>Food</u> is something you eat. Food can also mean something to think about.

Read the words in the carrot. Write them in the stew pot if they name "Food
for Eating." Write them in the wolf's head if they name "Food for Thought."
Add your own words, too!

carrot   idea   potato   peas   friendship   lesson

_____

_____

_____

_____

_____

_____

Name _____

DICTIONARY Put the words in ABC order to make the table of contents for a cookbook.

Contents

_____ 4

_____ 5

_____ 9

_____ 12

Page 2

Contents

_____ 20

_____ 26

_____ 30

_____ 35

Page 3

Contents

Page 2

Hamburger

Applesauce

Muffins

Bread

Page 3

Salad

Potatoes

Noodles

Yams

WORD SEARCH Look at the picture. Find five Spelling Words. Write them under the picture.

_____ _____ _____ _____ _____

SIDEWALKS SING "The Wolf's Chicken Stew" • Harcourt Brace School Publishers

Words with Long e, i, and o

Spelling WORDS

1. by
2. told
3. me
4. try
5. kind
6. cold
7. my
8. most
9. child
10. both

YOUR OWN WORDS

Look for other words with the long e, long i, or long o sounds. Write them here.

11. _____

12. _____

Each Spelling Word has the long <u>e</u>, long <u>i</u>, or long <u>o</u> sound. Look at the letters that spell those sounds.

Write the words in a way that will help you remember them.

why
by
try
my

mild
kind
child

post
told
cold
most
both

be
me

The long <u>e</u> sound can be spelled <u>e</u>.

The long <u>o</u> sound can be spelled <u>o</u>.

The long <u>i</u> sound can be spelled <u>i</u> or <u>y</u>.

SIDEWALKS SING "Everett Anderson's Friend" • Harcourt Brace School Publishers

Integrated Spelling

Name _Anthony_

STRATEGY Workshop

PROOFREADING: Checking Spelling Read what you wrote. Are all the words spelled correctly? Circle words you are not sure of. Check the spelling.

Which words do not look right? Circle the word in each pair that is misspelled. Write it correctly.

1. cold (moste) _most_   2. (trie) my _try_

3. (boath) by _both_   4. kind (tolde) _told_

Proofread this note. Circle the four words that are misspelled. Write them correctly.

Welcome to mye ___my___ apartment building. The people here are very kynd ___kind___. Please stop bie ___by___ to see mee ___me___.

Everett

Fun with Words Find a Spelling Word to fit the clues.

5. I rhyme with <u>wild</u>.
   I am the opposite of a grown-up.
   child

6. I rhyme with <u>fold</u>.
   I am the opposite of <u>hot</u>.
   cold

SIDEWALKS SING "Everett Anderson's Friend" • Harcourt Brace School Publishers

Name _____

VOCABULARY WordShop

Use Words to Explore to tell about the picture.

We are having _____ for dinner.

Some of the people are friends.

Some are part of my _____ .

I know them all. They are _____ to me.

My favorite _____ is here.

I will be the only boy. I will still have lots of fun!

Words to Explore

family

company

uncle

familiar

What's in a Word?

In English it's <u>boy</u>. In Spanish it's <u>muchacho</u>.
In French it's <u>garçon</u>, and in German it's <u>Junge</u>.

What are some other words for
<u>boy</u>? Write the words. Add one
of your own.

guy   kid   fellow

_____   _____

_____   _____

SIDEWALKS SING "Everett Anderson's Friend" • Harcourt Brace School Publishers

Integrated Spelling

SIDEWALKS SING "Everett Anderson's Friend" • Harcourt Brace School Publishers

Name _____

ANTONYMS Use a Spelling Word to write the opposite of each underlined word.

Friends

Friends are <u>mean</u> _____ .

I like mine.

My friend is a <u>grown-up</u> _____ .

We play outside when it's mild.

We play outside when it's <u>hot</u> _____ .

Because we are not too old!

I like my friend—A LOT!

ACTION WORDS Look at the friends in the pictures. Write an action word to tell what they are doing.

riding   reading   throwing

_____   _____   _____

WITH A FRIEND Use four Spelling Words to make a word search puzzle. Write the words across or down. Fill in the empty spaces with other letters. Then trade papers and find the words.

Integrated Spelling

Name _Anthony_

Words Like may and wait

Spelling WORDS

1. may
2. rain
3. say
4. wait
5. pay
6. train
7. lay
8. laid
9. way
10. tail

YOUR OWN WORDS

Look for other words with the long <u>a</u> sound. Write them here.

11. Clay
12. snake

Each Spelling Word has the long <u>a</u> sound. Look at the letters that spell that sound.

Write the words in a way that will help you remember them.

bay
say
pay
may
lay
way

paid
rain
wait
train
laid
tail

The long <u>a</u> sound can be spelled <u>ay</u> or <u>ai</u>.

SIDEWALKS SING "Mitchell Is Moving" • Harcourt Brace School Publishers

Name Anthony

STRATEGY Workshop

SPELLING STRATEGY: Rhyming Words Think about how to spell a rhyming word you know. Try that spelling. Does it look right?

Write five Spelling Words that rhyme with <u>day</u>. Circle the letters that are the same in each word.

day

may   Say   pay   way   Cay

Finish the poem with Spelling Words.

The Squirrel's Song

What a pain

To be caught in the ___rain___ .

I'll make a sail

With the help of my ___tail___ .

Fun with Words Write Spelling Words to tell what the chicken says.

I ___wait___ .

I get on the ___train___ .

I ___laid___ my egg!

SIDEWALKS SING "Mitchell Is Moving" • Harcourt Brace School Publishers

Integrated Spelling

VOCABULARY WordShop

Use a Word to Explore to complete the directions.

Words to Explore
. . . .
package

gigantic

tape

problem

How to Wrap a Big Box

1. Get enough paper to cover the _____.

2. Fold the paper, and _____ the ends.

3. Get a _____ string to go around the sides.

4. If you have a _____, ask a friend for help.

What's in a Word?

Mitchell is a dinosaur. <u>Dinosaur</u> comes from two Greek words that mean "terrible lizard."

Put the word parts together to name some dinosaurs.

stego + saurus   tyranno + saurus   apato + saurus

_____   _____   _____

SIDEWALKS SING "Mitchell Is Moving" • Harcourt Brace School Publishers

Name _____

NOUNS In "Mitchell Is Moving," Mitchell moved away. Look at this map. It shows things he might have seen on his way. Use nouns from the box to complete the key.

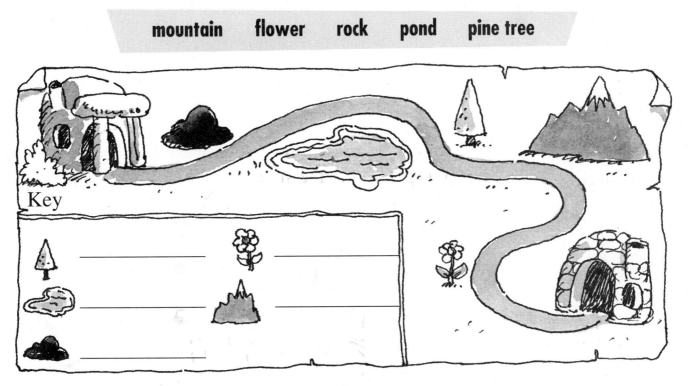

mountain   flower   rock   pond   pine tree

Key

TRY THIS When Mitchell moved, he brought Spelling Words with the <u>ay</u> spelling of long <u>a</u>. Margo brought Spelling Words with the <u>ai</u> spelling. Write each dinosaur's Spelling Words where they belong.

Mitchell   **Margo**

SIDEWALKS SING "Mitchell Is Moving" • Harcourt Brace School Publishers

Integrated Spelling

Name _____

Words Like keep and team

1. need
2. read
3. deep
4. eat
5. keep
6. team
7. feet
8. each
9. feel
10. seat

YOUR OWN WORDS

Look for other words with the long e sound. Write them here.

11. _____
12. _____

Each Spelling Word has the long e sound. Look at the letters that spell that sound.

Write the words in two groups to help you remember them.

meet

_____
_____
_____
_____
_____

neat

_____
_____
_____
_____

The long e sound can be spelled ee or ea.

SIDEWALKS SING "Jamaica Tag-Along" • Harcourt Brace School Publishers

STRATEGY Workshop

SPELLING CLUES: Spelling Rules Think about the ways long <u>e</u> can be spelled. Try different spellings until the word looks right. Check the spelling.

Write the correct spelling for each word.

1. deep   dep   _____

2. need   nead   _____

3. rede   read   _____

4. eet   eat   _____

Use Spelling Words to finish the rules. Write the correct spelling.

Basketball Rules

1. Remember that (eech, each) _____ player is important.

2. (Keep, Keap) _____ your eye on the ball.

3. Bounce the ball when you move your (fete, feet) _____.

4. Stay in your (seet, seat) _____ when not playing.

5. Play as a (team, teme) _____

Schedule

read

rea____

re____l

____eel

Fun with Words Start with the Spelling Word <u>read</u>. Change one letter each time. What Spelling Word do you get? Use it in a sentence.

SIDEWALKS SING "Jamaica Tag-Along" • Harcourt Brace School Publishers

Name _____

Use a Word to Explore to tell about
the basketball game.

Words to Explore
....
toss

toward

fair

shoot

_____ the ball to me!

Run _____ the basket!

Try to _____ now!

That isn't _____ .

What's in a Word?

Basketball is made up of two words, basket and ball. In basketball, you throw balls through a basket.

Use the clues to write the names for other sports.

You can kick this
ball with your
foot.

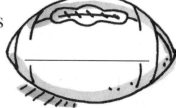

You hit a
ball and then
run to first base.

SIDEWALKS SING "Jamaica Tag-Along" • Harcourt Brace School Publishers

Integrated Spelling

Name _____

CLASSIFYING WORDS Write a Spelling Word that belongs in each group. Then add a word of your own.

Sports Words

basketball

player

_____

_____

Food Words

hungry

apple

_____

_____

Body Words

eyes

ears

_____

_____

DICTIONARY Write each group of story words in ABC order.

1. Ossie _____

Berto _____

Jamaica _____

2. castle _____

basketball _____

friend _____

SIDEWALKS SING "Jamaica Tag-Along" • Harcourt Brace School Publishers

Name Anthony

Words Like boat and show

Spelling WORDS

1. boat
2. row
3. show
4. coal
5. coat
6. slow
7. coast
8. own
9. low
10. road

YOUR OWN WORDS

Look for other words with the long o sound. Write them here.

11. _____
12. _____

Each Spelling Word has the long o sound. Look at the letters that spell the sound.

Write the words in two groups to help you remember them.

toad

coast
boat
road
coat
coal

mow

row
show
slow
own
low

The long o sound can be spelled oa or ow.

SIDEWALKS SING "Abuela" • Harcourt Brace School Publishers

Name Anthony

![STRATEGY Workshop]

PROOFREADING: Checking Spelling Read what you wrote. Do any words look funny? Circle them. Then check the spelling.

Which word in each pair is misspelled? Circle it. Then write it correctly.

1. (coale)   show   _coal_   2. row   (rowd)   _road_

3. boat   (sloa)   _slow_   4. (coate)   coast   _coat_

Circle the words that are misspelled. Write them correctly to complete the letter.

Dear Abuela,

    I loved our adventure. Do you remember the bowt _boat_ we saw? Well, I got to roa _row_ one of my oan _own_ !

The next time you visit, I will take you to the coste _coast_ and showe _show_ you how well I can row!

                Love, Rosa

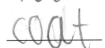

Fun with Words Find the Spelling Word hidden in these words. Write it in the shape.

_b l o w_

glow

blow

flow

SIDEWALKS SING "Abuela" • Harcourt Brace School Publishers

Integrated Spelling

Name _____

VOCABULARY WordShop

Write a Word to Explore under each picture.
Use the shapes to help you.

Words to Explore
· · · · · · · · · ·
above
adventure
glide
soar

1. [____][____][____][____]

2. [____][____][____][____]

3. [____][____][____][____]

Write a sentence about the bird's adventure. Use the word <u>adventure</u> in your sentence.

_____

_____

CITY WORDS Pretend you are a bird. You are
flying over New York City. What might you
see? Label the pictures to show.

people   train
statue   building

4. _____   5. _____   6. _____   7. _____

SIDEWALKS SING "Abuela" • Harcourt Brace School Publishers

Integrated Spelling

Name _____

What's in a Word?

Banana, burro, and abuela are all Spanish words.

Write each word under its picture.

_____ _____ _____

SYNONYMS Did you guess that abuela means "grandma" in Spanish? What are some other words for grandma? Write them around the picture.

_____   _____

_____   _____

WITH A PARTNER Cut out twelve clouds. Write one of these letters on each cloud: b, o, a, t, c, l, s, w, n, r, d, and h. Use your clouds to spell each Spelling Word. Then use each word in a sentence about flying in the sky. You will say ten sentences.

Integrated Spelling   **Lesson 10   49**

SIDEWALKS SING "Abuela" • Harcourt Brace School Publishers

Name Anthony

Practice Test

A. Read each sentence. Is the underlined word in the sentence spelled right or wrong? Mark your answer.

	Right	Wrong
1. My friends and I like to <u>jamp</u> rope.	○	●
2. We try to be <u>kind</u> to each other.	●	○
3. I <u>wate</u> for Susan after school.	●	✕
4. I <u>eat</u> lunch with my pal Peter.	●	○
5. In the winter, we <u>coast</u> on our sleds.	●	○
6. The school <u>bas</u> picks up fifty kids.	○	●
7. <u>Most</u> of my friends are second graders.	●	○

SIDEWALKS SING Unit 2 Review • Harcourt Brace School Publishers

Integrated Spelling

Name Anthony

B. Read each sentence. Is the underlined word in the sentence spelled right or wrong? Mark your answer.

	Right	Wrong
1. We <u>may</u> play ball on Saturday.	●	○
2. I <u>feal</u> good about my friends.	○	●
3. Putting on a <u>sho</u> with a friend is fun.	○	●
4. We <u>cat</u> hats from a newspaper.	●	⊘
5. My best friend <u>tolde</u> me a secret.	○	●
6. We splash through puddles in the <u>rain</u>.	●	○
7. We swing together on the <u>low</u> bars.	●	○
8. We see <u>eech</u> other every day.	○	●

SIDEWALKS SING Unit 2 Review • Harcourt Brace School Publishers

Integrated Spelling

Name _____

Words to Watch For

always

am

brother

father

mother

writing

DEAR FRIEND

Write a friendly letter to someone who lives in another place. It can be a real friend or an imaginary one. It can be a cousin or another relative. Tell the friend something about yourself or your class. Then ask the friend about herself or himself.

_____

_____

_____

_____

_____

_____

_____

TIPS FOR SPELLING SUCCESS Make sure that all your statements begin with a capital letter and end with a period. Make sure that all your questions begin with a capital letter and end with a question mark. Check to see that the names of people and places begin with a capital letter and are spelled correctly.

SIDEWALKS SING Unit 2 Review • Harcourt Brace School Publishers

COME FOR SUPPER

Pretend you could invite a character from a story you have read to supper. What would you talk about? Write down some questions you would ask. Then write a menu and a list of games to play. Choose food and games that you and your friend would both like.

TIPS FOR SPELLING SUCCESS Make sure that all your questions end with a question mark. Check your writing and your spelling.

WORD DOODLES

Use the clues to make new words.

1. Add a letter or letters to make a word.

   The ___ __a__ __i__ __n__ sounds like "drip-drop."

   The ___ ___ __a__ __i__ __n__ sounds like "choo choo."

2. Add the first and last letters to make a word.

   Take off your ___ __o__ __a__ ___.

   Walk down a ___ __o__ __a__ ___.

TIPS FOR SPELLING SUCCESS Use what you know about long vowel sounds to help you spell new words.

SIDEWALKS SING Unit 2 Review • Harcourt Brace School Publishers

Name Anthony

Words Like make and five

Spelling WORDS

1. take
2. fire
3. made
4. five
5. game
6. life
7. late
8. nice
9. make
10. side

YOUR OWN WORDS

Look for other words with the long a or the long i sound. Write them here.

11. nay
12. tide

Each Spelling Word has the long a or the long i sound. Look at the letters that spell those sounds.

Write the words in two groups to help you remember them.

same

take
made
game
late
make

like

fire
five
life
nice
side

The long a sound can be spelled a-consonant-e.

The long i sound can be spelled i-consonant-e.

Integrated Spelling

SIDEWALKS SING "Six-Dinner Sid" • Harcourt Brace School Publishers

Name Anthony

STRATEGY Workshop

SPELLING CLUES: Sounds and Letters Think about the letters that stand for the sounds you hear. Write the word. Does it look correct?

Choose the correct spelling for the Spelling Words. Write the words correctly.

1. (life) (lif) _life_ 2. fyre (fire) _fire_

3. mak (make) _make_ 4. (game) gam _game_

Use Spelling Words to finish this dinner invitation from one cat to another. Write the correct spelling.

Dear Tabby,

Please come for dinner tomorrow. I have (mead, made) _made_ a great cake. Dinner is at (fiv, five) _five_ o'clock. (Tak, Take) _take_ the bus. It will be so (nice, nyce) _nice_ to see you. Don't be (loat, late) _late_.

Your pal,
Calico

Fun with Words Tell about the picture. Add a letter to the cat's name to make it a Spelling Word.

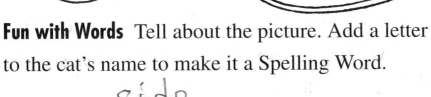

Sid is on his _side_ .

Integrated Spelling

SIDEWALKS SING "Six-Dinner Sid" • Harcourt Brace School Publishers

VOCABULARY WordShop

Use a Word to Explore to tell about each picture.

Words
to Explore
· · · · · · · · · · · · · ·
caught
discover
cough
medicine

1. My cat has

   a _____.

2. Call the vet to

   _____ what

   is wrong.

3. The vet says my

   cat has _____

   a cold.

4. She gives my cat

   some _____.

What's in a Word?

In the story "Six-Dinner Sid," Sid was a cat. Sid thought having six dinners every day was <u>the cat's meow</u>. <u>The cat's meow</u> means "just great." Sid was happy until the vet <u>let the cat out of the bag</u>. Did the vet have Sid in a bag? NO! To <u>let the cat out of the bag</u> means "to tell a secret."

5. What do <u>you</u> think is <u>the cat's meow</u>? _____

   _____

6. How do you think the vet <u>let the cat out of the bag</u>? _____

   _____

SIDEWALKS SING "Six-Dinner Sid" • Harcourt Brace School Publishers

Name _____

DESCRIBING WORDS Write a word from the box to describe each of the cats.
Then write a word of your own to describe each cat.

| sneaky | colorful | playful | sleepy |

_____   _____

_____

_____   _____

_____

TRY THIS! Write each group of Spelling Words in ABC order. If the first
letters are the same in both words, look at the second letters.

game _____   nice _____

five _____   side _____

life _____   make _____

late _____   life _____

SIDEWALKS SING "Six-Dinner Sid" • Harcourt Brace School Publishers

Words Like note and cute

Spelling WORDS

1. bone
2. mule
3. nose
4. huge
5. use
6. note
7. rope
8. cute
9. woke
10. hope

Look for other words with the long o or the long u sound. Write them here.

11. _____
12. _____

Each Spelling Word has the long o or the long u sound. Look at the letters that spell those sounds.

Write the words in two groups to help you remember them.

home

bone
nose
note
rope
woke
hope

fuse

mule
huge
use
cute

The long o sound can be spelled o-consonant-e.

The long u sound can be spelled u-consonant-e.

SIDEWALKS SING "Old Henry" • Harcourt Brace School Publishers

Integrated Spelling

STRATEGY Workshop

SPELLING CLUES: Rhyming Words Think about rhyming words. Try spelling the word like a rhyming word you know. Does it look right?

Write a Spelling Word to rhyme with each word. Then circle the letters that are the same in each word.

1. fuse _use_

2. rose _nose_

3. phone _bone_

4. poke _woke_

Use a Spelling Word to complete each rhyme.

Henry wrote a little _note_.

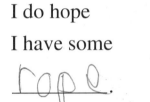

I do hope
I have some _rope_.

Fun with Words Find these Spelling Words and circle them:

huge   mule
hope   cute

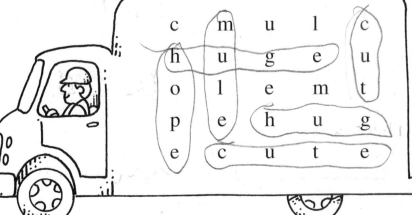

c	m	u	l	c
h	u	g	e	u
o	l	e	m	t
p	e	h	u	g
e	c	u	t	e

SIDEWALKS SING "Old Henry" • Harcourt Brace School Publishers

Name Anthony

Complete the entries from Henry's diary. Write a Word to Explore in each shape.

October

The [p][e][o][p][l][e] formed a committee.

They asked me to [m][o][v][e] out.

November

I packed my bags. I made a [p][l][a][n] to leave.

May

I missed my house. I wrote a note to the mayor. I asked about going home.

I hope he will [d][e][c][i][d][e] soon.

Words to Explore

decide

plan

move

people

SEASONS A house can look different in each season. Look at each picture. Write the name of the season under it.

autumn   spring   winter   summer

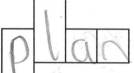

1. Winter   2. autumn   3. Summer

4. Which season is left? Spring

SIDEWALKS SING "Old Henry" • Harcourt Brace School Publishers

Integrated Spelling

Name Anthony

What's in a Word?

A <u>house</u> is a building, but a <u>home</u> can be any place where a person or an animal chooses to live.

Write the name for each home. Then write who might live there.

house
nest
hive
den
burrow

nest
bird

hive
bee

house
child

den
wolf

burrow
snake

WORD SEARCH Look at the picture. Find pictures of five Spelling Words. Write them under the picture.

note mule bone nose rope

SIDEWALKS SING "Old Henry" • Harcourt Brace School Publishers

Consonant Clusters

Spelling WORDS

1. from
2. dry
3. still
4. fast
5. blow
6. grass
7. sled
8. stood
9. last
10. fly

Look for other words with consonant clusters. Write them here.

11. blend
12. sports

Each Spelling Word has a consonant cluster. Look at the letters that spell the consonant clusters. Do you see the clusters with l, r, and t?

Write the Spelling Words in groups to help you remember them.

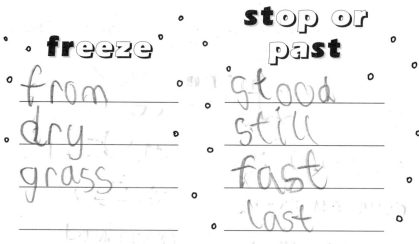

freeze
from
dry
grass

stop or past
stood
still
fast
last

play
fly
sled
blow

The letters l, r, and t can be parts of consonant clusters.

SIDEWALKS SING "Little Penguin's Tale" • Harcourt Brace School Publishers

STRATEGY Workshop

SPELLING CLUES: Rhyming Words Think of rhyming words. Then spell the word like a rhyming word you know. Does it look right?

Circle the two rhyming words. Then write the Spelling Word.

1. (cast) land (last)   _last_   2. (grass) (brass) grape   _grass_

3. drip (dry) (try)   _dry_   4. (stood) said (hood)   _stood_

Write a rhyming Spelling Word to complete the ad.

Come to the Land of Ice and Snow

Rent a (bed) _sled_. (My) _Fly_ down a snowy hill as (last) _fast_ as you can go. Then hear the wind (glow) _blow_. You won't want to sit (hill) _still_! You'll want to go, go, go!

Fun with Words Write a Spelling Word to tell about the penguin.

SOUTH POLE

I am a penguin _from_ the South Pole.

SIDEWALKS SING "Little Penguin's Tale" • Harcourt Brace School Publishers

Name _____

VOCABULARY WordShop

Use Words to Explore to tell about the picture.

Words to Explore
....
gather
join
tune
play

The pigs _____ to _____ a merry _____ .

The penguins _____ the other dancers.

CLASSIFYING Some animals can fly and others can swim. Write the animals that fly in the bird. Write the animals that swim in the whale. Then add two other animals that fit.

| bird | whale | shark | bat | duck | penguin |

SIDEWALKS SING "Little Penguin's Tale" • Harcourt Brace School Publishers

Integrated Spelling

SIDEWALKS SING "Little Penguin's Tale" • Harcourt Brace School Publishers

Name _____

What's in a Word?

Have you ever read a <u>tale</u> about a penguin who lost his <u>tail</u>? Sometimes words sound the same but are spelled differently and have different meanings.

Write the correct words under the pictures. Then add two words of your own. Draw a picture for each word.

tale
tail
hare
hair

_____   _____   _____   _____

_____   _____

DICTIONARY Put each group of words in ABC order to make sentences. Remember to use capital letters and periods.

Penguin Little slept _____

too played Little Penguin _____

Nanny Grand Penguin you told _____

_____

WITH A PARTNER Choose five Spelling Words. Write them on cards. Cut the letters apart to make puzzles. Put the words back together.

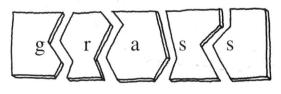

Integrated Spelling

Final Double Consonants

SIDEWALKS SING "Fiesta!" • Harcourt Brace School Publishers

Spelling WORDS

1. ball
2. add
3. miss
4. all
5. dress
6. fall
7. less
8. call
9. pass
10. glass

YOUR OWN WORDS

Look for other words with final double consonants. Write them here.

11. stress
12. doll

Each Spelling Word ends with a double consonant. Look at the letters that spell the ending sounds.

Write the Spelling Words in groups to help you remember them.

OK

grass

miss
dress
less
pass
glass

tall

ball
all
fall
call

What word is left? __add__

Words can have final double consonants with <u>d</u>, <u>l</u>, and <u>s</u>.

penguin polar

Name _Anthony_

OK

PROOFREADING: Check Spelling Does every word look right? Circle words you are not sure of. Then check the spelling in a dictionary.

Circle the word that is spelled incorrectly. Write it correctly.

1. (cal) ball _call_

2. add (les) _less_

3. (mis) all _miss_

4. (pas) dress _pass_

Find the incorrectly spelled words in the recipe. Write them correctly.

Flour Tortillas

- Gather al _all_ the ingredients.
- Mix flour, salt, and baking soda.
- Ad _add_ oil and water.
- Make one dough bal _ball_ at a time.
- Roll each one out and cook.

Fun with Words Unscramble the letters in each picture to write a Spelling Word.

5. _dress_

6. _glass_

7. _fall_

Integrated Spelling

SIDEWALKS SING "Fiesta!" • Harcourt Brace School Publishers

Name _____

VOCABULARY WordShop

Look at the pictures. Write a Word to Explore to complete each sentence.

Words **to Explore**

· · · · · · · · · · · · · ·

celebrate

festival

important

fiesta

1. Welcome to the _____! 2. Today is an _____ day.

3. We are going to _____. 4. We sing and dance at the _____.

MUSICAL NOUNS Use one of these music words to label each musical instrument that you might hear at a festival.

5. _____

6. _____

guitar

maracas

trumpet

violin

7. _____

8. _____

SIDEWALKS SING "Fiesta!" • Harcourt Brace School Publishers

Integrated Spelling

What's in a Word?

Fiesta is a Spanish word. It means "festival" or "celebration." What are some things you celebrate?

Draw a picture of your celebration. Write a sentence about it.

_____

_____

TRY THIS! Use Spelling Words to complete the puzzle. Then make a puzzle of your own.

Across

2. opposite of <u>subtract</u>

3. opposite of <u>more</u>

Down

1. a bouncing toy

4. something to wear

SIDEWALKS SING "Fiesta!" • Harcourt Brace School Publishers

Words with sh and ch

Spelling WORDS

1. ship
2. rich
3. wash
4. change
5. shop
6. chest
7. fish
8. reach
9. wish
10. shape

YOUR OWN WORDS

Look for other words with the sh or the ch sound. Write them here.

11. favorite
12. balloon

Each Spelling Word has the letters sh or ch. Look at each word. Where do you see sh or ch?

Write the words in four groups to help you remember them.

shoe
Ship
shop
shape

dish
wash
fish
wish

child
change
chest

peach
reach
rich

The sh sound can be spelled sh.

The ch sound can be spelled ch.

SIDEWALKS SING "Miss Eva and the Red Balloon" • Harcourt Brace School Publishers

Integrated Spelling

STRATEGY Workshop

SPELLING RULES: Sounds and Letters Listen for the sounds. Then write the letters that stand for the sounds.

Add <u>sh</u> or <u>ch</u> to each word. Then write the Spelling Word.

1. fi __sh__   _fish_

2. wa __sh__   _wash_

3. ri __ch__   _rich_

4. wi __sh__   _wish_

Finish the story. Add an <u>sh</u> or a <u>ch</u> to complete each underlined Spelling Word. Then write the word.

Magic Nights

I have a toy __ch__est in my room. Every night after the lights are out, I rea__ch__ into it. That is when my toys seem to __ch__ange . The dolls dance and even change __sh__ape . In the morning, all is quiet. Only one doll winks before she goes to sleep.

Fun with Words Write a Spelling Word to tell about each picture.

5. _ship_

6. _shop_

SIDEWALKS SING "Miss Eva and the Red Balloon" • Harcourt Brace School Publishers

Name _____

VOCABULARY WordShop

Write Words to Explore to answer the party riddles.

SIDEWALKS SING "Miss Eva and the Red Balloon" • Harcourt Brace School Publishers

Words
to Explore
. . . .
favorite

balloon

brought

round

1. You blow me up. What am I?

   _____

2. Be careful or I will pop. What shape am I?

   _____

3. I tell about one thing you like best.

   What word am I? _____

4. How did the present get to the party?

   You _____ it!

DICTIONARY Complete the dictionary page. Write the Words to Explore in ABC order.

_____

_____

_____

_____

Name _____

What's in a Word?

Some people blow out the candles and make a <u>wish</u>. Other people make a <u>wish</u> upon a star.

What do you wish for? Write sentences to tell.

I wish . . .

_____

_____

_____

_____

_____

_____

TRY THIS! Under each word shape, write the Spelling Words that fit the shape.

1. _____

   _____

2. _____

   _____

3. _____

4. _____

SIDEWALKS SING "Miss Eva and the Red Balloon" • Harcourt Brace School Publishers

Name

Practice Test

A. Look at the three spelling choices for each word. Choose the correct one. Mark the letter for that word.

1. A fier   B fire   C frie   1. (A) (B) (C)

2. A mak   B mac   C make   2. (A) (B) (C)

3. A mule   B mul   C mol   3. (A) (B) (C)

4. A dres   B dress   C driss   4. (A) (B) (C)

5. A fli   B fly   C flie   5. (A) (B) (C)

6. A reche   B reach   C reatch   6. (A) (B) (C)

7. A knose   B nos   C nose   7. (A) (B) (C)

SIDEWALKS SING Unit 3 Review • Harcourt Brace School Publishers

Integrated Spelling

B. Look at the three spelling choices for each word. Choose the correct one. Mark the letter for that word.

1. Ⓐ rich
   Ⓑ riche
   Ⓒ rish

2. Ⓐ nic
   Ⓑ nice
   Ⓒ nise

3. Ⓐ bal
   Ⓑ ball
   Ⓒ baol

4. Ⓐ lat
   Ⓑ laet
   Ⓒ late

5. Ⓐ glass
   Ⓑ glas
   Ⓒ glase

6. Ⓐ blowe
   Ⓑ bloe
   Ⓒ blow

7. Ⓐ uze
   Ⓑ use
   Ⓒ usse

8. Ⓐ five
   Ⓑ fiv
   Ⓒ fieve

SIDEWALKS SING Unit 3 Review • Harcourt Brace School Publishers

Name _____

Words to Watch For

and

balloon

cousin

house

make

Thanksgiving

HOLIDAY RHYME

Choose a holiday to write a poem about. Think of the reasons the holiday is special to you. Think of why you celebrate it, what you wear, and what you eat. Think about music. Think about decorations. Think about the people with whom you celebrate the holiday. Now make some notes for your poem. Write down rhyming words or phrases that will show the spirit of the holiday.

TIPS FOR SPELLING SUCCESS Be sure to capitalize names, places, months, and holidays. Read your poem again and look for spelling errors.

SIDEWALKS SING Unit 3 Review • Harcourt Brace School Publishers

SIDEWALKS SING Unit 3 Review • Harcourt Brace School Publishers

Name _____

GUIDED TOUR

Suppose you could visit the neighborhood in one of the stories you have read. What would you do there? What would you see? Make a map of that neighborhood. Draw and label the special places you would visit. Make up street names. Add houses and stores. Think about what you would talk about if you were giving someone a tour.

TIPS FOR SPELLING SUCCESS Make sure that the streets and place names begin with capital letters. Check for spelling errors.

WORD DOODLES

Use the clues to make words.

1. Add a consonant or consonants to make a phrase that means <u>hot on the shore</u>.

   <u>h</u> <u>e</u> <u>a</u> __ on the <u>b</u> <u>e</u> <u>a</u> __ __

2. Add an <u>i</u> or an <u>e</u> to make a phrase that means <u>step over a spill</u>.

   <u>m</u> __ <u>s</u> <u>s</u> the <u>m</u> __ <u>s</u> <u>s</u>

TIPS FOR SPELLING SUCCESS Use what you know about how consonants sound alone and with other consonants to help you spell new words.

Words with th, wh, and ng

Spelling WORDS

1. _long_
2. _they_
3. _which_
4. _bath_
5. _ring_
6. _them_
7. _while_
8. _math_
9. _those_
10. _than_

YOUR OWN WORDS

Look for other words with the th, wh, or ng sound. Write them here.

11. _fling_
12. _when_

Each Spelling Word has the th, the wh, or the ng sound. Look at the letters that spell each sound.

Write the Spelling Words in four groups to help you remember them.

path
bath
math

that
they
them
those
than

sing
long
ring

when
which
while

Words can have the th sound at the beginning or the end.

Words can have the wh sound at the beginning.

Words can have the ng sound at the end.

burrow stretch

ALL KINDS OF FRIENDS "Awful Aardvark" • Harcourt Brace School Publishers

Integrated Spelling

Name _Anthony_

STRATEGY Workshop

SPELLING CLUES: Sounds and Letters Listen for the sounds and think about how to spell them. Write the word. Does it look right?

Listen for the sounds. Then write the spelling that looks right.

1. (while) yile _while_
2. (ring) rin _ring_
3. han (than) _than_
4. mah (math) _math_

Complete the sentences about your favorite animals. Think about the sounds to help you write the Spelling Word correctly.

5. (Wich, Which) _Which_ animals are these?

6. (They, Tey) _they_ are aardvarks.

7. Look at their (long, lon) _long_ noses!

8. What do aardvarks do with (tose, those) _those_?

Fun with Words Do word math.

Write the Spelling Word.

9. bag – g + them – e – m = _bath_

10. that – at + e + my – y = _them_

ALL KINDS OF FRIENDS "Awful Aardvark" • Harcourt Brace School Publishers

Name _____

VOCABULARY WordShop

Use Words to Explore to tell about the pictures.

Words to Explore

stretch

angry

awful

snore

Lion likes to _____.

Aardvark likes to _____.

That makes Lion _____.

Snoring makes an _____ sound!

What's in a Word?

Aardvark comes from a Dutch word that means "earth pig." An aardvark is an African anteater. Why do you think people called aardvarks "earth pigs"?

Write a sentence. Tell what you think. _____

_____

ALL KINDS OF FRIENDS "Awful Aardvark" • Harcourt Brace School Publishers

Integrated Spelling

Name _____

CLASSIFYING Look at each group of animals pictured. Decide how the animals are alike. Write the words that tell how they are alike.

1. _____

2. _____

DICTIONARY Write these three Spelling Words in ABC order. The words begin with the same two letters, so look at the third letter.

they   than   those

  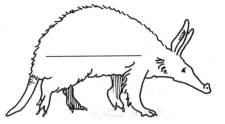

3. _____   _____   _____

ON YOUR OWN Draw a picture of two animals you know or like. Then choose five Spelling Words. Use them to write sentences about your picture.

Integrated Spelling   **Lesson 18   81**

ALL KINDS OF FRIENDS "Awful Aardvark" • Harcourt Brace School Publishers

Words Like car, book, and track

Spelling WORDS

1. car
2. book
3. stick
4. kick
5. took
6. care
7. track
8. black
9. neck
10. pack

YOUR OWN WORDS

Look for other words with the k sound. Write them here.

11. Clay
12. Connolly

Each Spelling Word has the k sound spelled k, c, or ck. Look at the letters that can spell this sound.

Write the Spelling Words in three groups to help you remember them.

look

book
took

can

car
care

lick

stick
kick
track
black
neck
pack

The k sound can be spelled k, c, or ck.

cozy milk **Integrated Spelling**

ALL KINDS OF FRIENDS "It's an Armadillo!" • Harcourt Brace School Publishers

Name _____

S T R A T E G Y Workshop

SPELLING CLUES: Sounds and Letters Think about letters that can spell the sounds. Try each letter or pair of letters. Does the word look right?

Add <u>k</u> or <u>ck</u> to complete each Spelling Word. Write the Spelling Words.

1. boo<u>k</u> _book_ ✗

2. ki<u>ck</u> _kick_

3. ne<u>ck</u> _neck_

4. too<u>k</u> _took_

Add letters to complete the Spelling Words. Then write the Spelling Words to tell about the pictures.

pa<u>ck</u>

sti<u>ck</u>

5. Put on a _pack_ .

6. Walk with a _stick_ .

tra<u>ck</u>

bla<u>ck</u>

7. See this animal _track_ .

8. It belongs to a _black_ bear.

Fun with Words Add a vowel to one Spelling Word to make another Spelling Word.

car

care

Integrated Spelling

Lesson 19 83

ALL KINDS OF FRIENDS "It's an Armadillo!" • Harcourt Brace School Publishers

Name _____

VOCABULARY WordShop

Imagine that you are a baby armadillo making a home. Fill in the chart with Words to Explore. Add your own ideas about other animals.

Words to Explore

cozy
milk
lively
burrow

Kind of Home	How It Feels	Food to Eat
burrow	cozy lively	milk

ANIMAL HOMES Complete the chart. Write the name of each animal home shown. Then write the name of the animal that lives there.

Animal Homes
cave
anthill
nest
burrow

Animals
armadillo
bear
bird
ant

	Home	Animal
	nest	bird
	cave	bear
	burrow	armadillo
	anthill	ant

84   Lesson 19

Integrated Spelling

ALL KINDS OF FRIENDS "It's an Armadillo!" • Harcourt Brace School Publishers

Name Anthony

What's in a Word?

Armadillo is a Spanish word. It means "little armored one." Here are some other Spanish words.

Write each word under its picture.

| banana | abuela | piñata | burro |

1. burro   2. abuela   3. piñata   4. banana

QUESTION WORDS Write question words to complete the questions. Then write words to answer them.

| What | Where | When |

5. What animal is in the picture? armadillo

6. Where is it sleeping? burrow

7. when does it go out? ✓

WITH A PARTNER Write the Spelling Words on cards. Then put them in ABC order. As you take turns reading each word, use it in a sentence about an armadillo or another animal you know about.

Integrated Spelling   **Lesson 19   85**

ALL KINDS OF FRIENDS "It's an Armadillo!" • Harcourt Brace School Publishers

Words Like she's and you're

ALL KINDS OF FRIENDS "The Day Jimmy's Boa Ate the Wash" • Harcourt Brace School Publishers

Spelling WORDS

1. he's
2. we're
3. I'm
4. she's
5. they're
6. I'll
7. you're
8. that's
9. there's
10. what's

YOUR OWN WORDS

Look for other contractions with is and will. Write them here.

11. it's
12. won't

Each Spelling Word is a contraction. Look at the letters that spell each word.

Write the contractions in four groups to help you remember them.

is
he's
she's
that's
there's
what's

are
we're
they're
you're

will
I'll

am
I'm

Contractions can be made by combining words with is, are, will, and am.

Integrated Spelling

Name Anthony

STRATEGY Workshop

SPELLING RULES: Contractions Think about the two words the contraction stands for. What letters have been left out? Write the contraction. Does it look right?

Write the contraction that stands for each pair of words.

1. they are ___they're___   2. you are ___you're___

3. she is ___she's___   4. that is ___that's___

Write contractions for the underlined words in the story.

Our Class Trip

We are ___We're___ going to visit a farm.

There is ___There's___ a lot to see.

The farmer will show us his animals.

He is ___He's___ going to show us how

he plants corn, too! I am ___I'm___ sure I

will have fun! What is ___What's___ your

favorite place to visit?

Fun with Words Use a Spelling Word to complete the sentence.

"I will have fun at the farm."

"___I'll___ have fun at the farm, too!"

ALL KINDS OF FRIENDS "The Day Jimmy's Boa Ate the Wash" • Harcourt Brace School Publishers

Integrated Spelling

VOCABULARY WordShop

Complete the diary entry. Use Words to Explore
to tell about the picture.

Dear Diary,

Today I visited a farm. The chickens were

_____ loudly. The kids were _____

eggs, and the puppy was running in circles.

But the farmer's wife was really screaming.

She got a little _____ when she saw a

boa in her wash. There's nothing _____

about life on a farm!

Words to Explore
. . . .
boring
excited
throwing
squawking

ACTION WORDS Write action words for the animal
in each picture. Add some of your own.

| hopping | galloping | slithering | hissing | croaking | neighing |

_____ _____ _____

_____ _____ _____

_____ _____ _____

ALL KINDS OF FRIENDS "The Day Jimmy's Boa Ate the Wash" • Harcourt Brace School Publishers

What's in a Word?

A farmer is "one who farms." A teacher is "one who teaches."

Write words for the following. Then draw a line from each word to its picture.

1. one who builds _____

2. one who sings _____

3. one who dances _____

4. one who bakes _____

DICTIONARY Write these snake names in ABC order.

| boa | rattlesnake | asp | cobra |

5. _____   _____   _____   _____

WITH A PARTNER Make word cards for the Spelling Words. Then make word cards for the two words each contraction stands for. Use your cards to play a matching game. Match each Spelling Word to the two words it stands for.

ALL KINDS OF FRIENDS "The Day Jimmy's Boa Ate the Wash" • Harcourt Brace School Publishers

Name Anthony Michael Connobby

Words Like food and new

Spelling WORDS

1. soon
2. grew
3. you
4. room
5. new
6. group
7. school
8. flew
9. food
10. drew

YOUR OWN WORDS

Look for other words with the same vowel sound. Write them here.

11. mammal
12. change

All the Spelling Words have the same vowel sound. Look at the letters—ew, oo, or ou—that can spell that sound.

Write the Spelling Words in three groups to help you remember them.

soup
group
you

boom
soon
room
school
food

blew
grew
new
flew
drew

Words with the /oo/ sound can be spelled oo, ew, or ou.

ALL KINDS OF FRIENDS "A Dinosaur Named After Me" • Harcourt Brace School Publishers

Integrated Spelling

Name _Anthony Michael Connolly_

STRATEGY Workshop

SPELLING CLUES: Sounds and Letters Sometimes one vowel sound can be spelled in different ways. Choose one way and write the word. Does it look right?

Write the correct spelling of each Spelling Word.

1. grou   grew   _grew_   2. soun   soon   _soon_

3. new   noo   _new_   4. grewp   group   _group_

Use Spelling Words to tell about the silly pictures.
Write the correct spelling of each word.

5. Stego likes (fewd, food) _food_.

6. Rex (drew, drou) _drew_.

7. Tera (flew, floo) _flew_.

8. The dinosaurs go to (schoul, school) _school_.

Fun with Words Write a Spelling Word to fit each clue.

9. I sound like a letter of the alphabet.

you

10. I'm part of a house.

room

 ALL KINDS OF FRIENDS "A Dinosaur Named Named After Me" • Harcourt Brace School Publishers

Name _____

VOCABULARY WordShop

Use Words to Explore to finish the report.

Words to Explore
. . . .

change

larger

member

mammal

Dinosaurs

Was a dinosaur a kind of reptile, bird, _____, or amphibian? The dinosaur was a _____ of the reptile group. Some dinosaurs ate only vegetables. Others ate meat. Some dinosaurs were _____ than a house. Scientists sometimes _____ the names of dinosaurs.

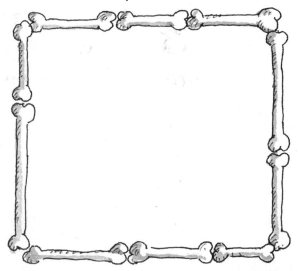

What's in a Word?

Pentaceratops was a dinosaur. <u>Pentaceratops</u> means "five-horned face." Triceratops was another dinosaur. <u>Tri</u> means "three."

1. What do you think <u>Triceratops</u>

   means? _____

2. What shape can you think of

   that begins with <u>tri</u>? _____

3. Draw a picture of one.

ALL KINDS OF FRIENDS "A Dinosaur Named After Me" • Harcourt Brace School Publishers

Name _____

SIZE WORDS Most dinosaurs were big animals. Mice are small animals. Write size words to complete each web. Add some of your own.

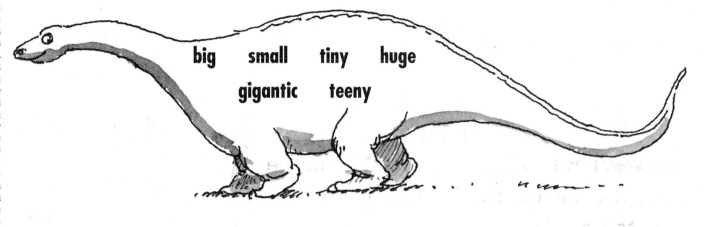

big   small   tiny   huge
gigantic   teeny

1. _____

2. _____   _____

_____   _____

_____

_____

CLASSIFYING Are the animals big or small? Write each animal name in the right place. Add animal names of your own.

rabbit   elephant   skunk    giraffe

Big   Small

_____   _____

_____   _____

_____   _____

ALL KINDS OF FRIENDS "A Dinosaur Named After Me" • Harcourt Brace School Publishers

Name _____

Words Like fight and sky

Spelling WORDS

1. high
2. cry
3. night
4. sky
5. fight
6. right
7. light
8. sight
9. bright
10. might

Look for other words with the long i sound. Write them here.

11. _____
12. _____

Each Spelling Word has the long i sound. Look at the letters that can spell the sound.

Write the Spelling Words in two groups to help you remember them.

tight

_____
_____
_____
_____
_____

my

_____
_____
_____

ALL KINDS OF FRIENDS "Tyrone the Horrible" • Harcourt Brace School Publishers

Integrated Spelling

Name _____

STRATEGY Workshop

SPELLING CLUES: Rhyming Words Think of rhyming words. Then spell the word like a rhyming word you know. Does it look right?

Circle the word that rhymes with the first word in each row. Then write the rhyming word.

1. why	sky	find	
2. fly	fit	cry	
3. light	bright	bit	
4. tight	mine	might	
5. fight	right	feet	

Write Spelling Words to complete the poem. Circle the letters that are the same.

The dinosaur looked up at the sky one _____.

He saw a bright and shining _____.

"Oh, my!" he exclaimed. "What a beautiful _____!"

light
night
sight

Fun with Words Unscramble the letters in each dinosaur to make a Spelling Word.

i h h g

_____

f t h
g i

_____

ALL KINDS OF FRIENDS "Tyrone the Horrible" • Harcourt Brace School Publishers

Name _____

VOCABULARY WordShop

Use words from the box to describe each picture.

Words to Explore
....
against

avoid

furious

trouble

This dinosaur is fighting _____ the other dinosaurs.

This dinosaur

is _____.

This dinosaur is

in big _____.

This dinosaur wants to

_____ getting caught.

DESCRIPTIONS Write your own word to describe this picture.

This dinosaur is _____.

ALL KINDS OF FRIENDS "Tyrone the Horrible" • Harcourt Brace School Publishers

Integrated Spelling

What's in a Word?

A Tyrannosaurus was a very fierce dinosaur. Tyrannosaur comes from Greek words meaning "tyrant lizard."

1. What do you think tyrant means? _____

2. Make up your own name for a fierce dinosaur.

_____

ANTONYMS The words fierce and gentle are opposites. Write a Spelling Word that is the opposite of each word.

3. day _____

4. dim _____

5. low _____

6. heavy _____

ON YOUR OWN Choose six Spelling Words. Use them to write rhymes about the night.

ALL KINDS OF FRIENDS "Tyrone the Horrible" • Harcourt Brace School Publishers

Name Anthony

Practice Test

A. Read each sentence. Find the correctly spelled word to complete it. Mark the letter next to that word.

1. My dog likes to take a _____ in the rain.
   - Ⓐ bathe
   - Ⓑ beth
   - Ⓒ bath

2. I like to _____ animals in the woods.
   - Ⓐ track
   - Ⓑ trak
   - Ⓒ trake

3. _____ not afraid of lizards or snakes.
   - Ⓐ Shes
   - Ⓑ She's
   - Ⓒ Shes'

4. The zookeeper visited our _____.
   - Ⓐ skol
   - Ⓑ schol
   - Ⓒ school

5. Bats are mammals that fly at _____.
   - Ⓐ night
   - Ⓑ nite
   - Ⓒ nigt

6. The bee stung me _____ I slept.
   - Ⓐ wile
   - Ⓑ while
   - Ⓒ whil

7. Wild dogs like to travel in a _____.
   - Ⓐ pak
   - Ⓑ pac
   - Ⓒ pack

ALL KINDS OF FRIENDS Unit 1 Review • Harcourt Brace School Publishers

Integrated Spelling

Name Anthony

B. Read each sentence. Find the correctly spelled word to complete it. Mark the letter next to that word.

1. _____ your favorite animal?

   (A) What's   (B) Wat's   (C) Whats

2. I _____ a picture of some dinosaurs.

   (A) drewe   (B) drew   (C) dreew

3. Some animals _____ over food.

   (A) fight   (B) fite   (C) fihte

4. Giraffes have very _____ necks.

   (A) long   (B) loong   (C) lon

5. I read a _____ about reptiles.

   (A) bok   (B) book   (C) boock

6. I think _____ get a puppy soon.

   (A) Ill   (B) I'll   (C) Ile

7. My parrot _____ right out the door.

   (A) flew   (B) fliw   (C) fleu

8. I _____ like to study animals someday.

   (A) mite   (B) mihgt   (C) might

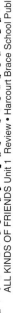

ALL KINDS OF FRIENDS Unit 1 Review • Harcourt Brace School Publishers

Name _____

Words to Watch For

didn't

dog

everybody

fun

know

that's

ANIMAL FUN

Write a funny story about an animal. It can be a real animal or an imaginary one. It can live at your house, at the zoo, or in the jungle. Think about why your story is funny. Then think about a beginning, a middle, and an ending. Write some notes here. What other animals or people are in the story? What is the order of the things that happen? Draw a cover for your story when it is finished. Don't forget a title.

Notes

_____
_____
_____
_____
_____

TIPS FOR SPELLING SUCCESS Make sure that all the plurals in your story are spelled correctly. Check to see that you started every sentence with a capital letter. Look up words in a dictionary if you are unsure of their spelling.

ALL KINDS OF FRIENDS Unit 1 Review • Harcourt Brace School Publishers

Welcome Home

Choose one of the animals that you have read about in class. Imagine what it would be like to have that animal live with you. How would you prepare for its arrival? Where would it live? What would it eat? Make a list of all the things you would need to welcome this animal into your home. Then make a "Welcome Home" banner and display it in your classroom.

TIPS FOR SPELLING SUCCESS Check your list to make sure you have spelled each word correctly. Use a dictionary if you are unsure.

WORD DOODLES

Use the clues to finish the rhymes. Add a letter or letters.

Read a <u>b</u> <u>o</u> <u>o</u> <u>K</u>,

By the  <u>b</u> <u>r</u> <u>o</u> <u>o</u> <u> </u>, OOPS!

Do your 2 + 3 = 5 <u>m</u> <u>a</u> <u>t</u> <u>h</u>,

Then take a <u>b</u> <u>a</u> <u>t</u> <u>h</u>.

TIPS FOR SPELLING SUCCESS Use what you know about how consonants sound at the end of words to help you spell new words.

ALL KINDS OF FRIENDS Unit 1 Review • Harcourt Brace School Publishers

Name _____

Words Like arm and heart

Spelling WORDS

1. arm
2. are
3. far
4. heart
5. dark
6. hard
7. farm
8. park
9. start
10. part

YOUR OWN WORDS

Look for other words with the same vowel sound. Write them here.

11. _____

12. _____

Each Spelling Word has the vowel sound heard in far. Look at the letters that spell that sound.

Write the Spelling Words in a way that will help you remember them.

charm

_____
_____
_____
_____
_____
_____
_____

art

_____
_____
_____

Which Spelling Word does not fit in a list?

_____

Words with the /är/ sound can be spelled ar or ear.

ALL KINDS OF FRIENDS "The Chalk Doll" • Harcourt Brace School Publishers

Integrated Spelling

STRATEGY Workshop

PROOFREADING: Check Spelling Read what you wrote. If you are not sure how a word is spelled, circle it. Then check the spelling.

Which words do not look right? Circle the misspelled word in each row. Write it correctly.

1. fa   are   heart   _____

2. part   peark   start   _____

3. hard   arm   deark   _____

4. art   fearm   cart   _____

Circle the misspelled words. Write them correctly.

I'm making a rag doll. I will

steart _____ with a basket of rags.

I will make peart _____ of my doll

blue. One earm _____ will be yellow!

I will sew on eyes, a nose, and a mouth. Then

I will sew on a big red hart _____.

Making a rag doll is not harde _____ at all!

Fun with Words Write the Spelling Word that sounds like a letter of the alphabet. _____

ALL KINDS OF FRIENDS "The Chalk Doll" • Harcourt Brace School Publishers

Name _____

VOCABULARY WordShop

Use Words to Explore to complete the directions
for making a rag doll.

Words to Explore

material
sewing
scissors
thread

1. Fold a piece of _____, and draw
   an outline of the doll.
2. Use _____ to cut out the shape.
3. Put _____ in your needle and sew.
4. When you are almost finished _____,
   stuff the doll with rags.

What's in a Word?

The word <u>doll</u> comes from a nickname for Dorothy. A doll is a toy that many children play with.

Write each toy name under its picture. Then draw a toy of your own and
label it.

robot   ball   game   blocks   train

5. _____   6. _____   7. _____

8. _____   9. _____   10. _____

ALL KINDS OF FRIENDS "The Chalk Doll" • Harcourt Brace School Publishers

Integrated Spelling

Name _____

MULTIPLE MEANINGS The word <u>material</u> can mean "sewing fabric." <u>Material</u> can also mean "what something is made of." List the materials under the correct heading in the outline.

Materials

Wheels	Paint	Thread	Cloth	Wood	Stuffing

Making Toys

1. Wagon

   A. _____

   B. _____

   C. _____

2. Rag Doll

   A. _____

   B. _____

   C. _____

WITH A PARTNER Cut out five paper-doll shapes. Write a Spelling Word on each doll. Then choose a doll. Read the word, and use it in a sentence.

ALL KINDS OF FRIENDS "The Chalk Doll" • Harcourt Brace School Publishers

Words Like door and more

ALL KINDS OF FRIENDS "The Little Painter of Sabana Grande" • Harcourt Brace School Publishers

Spelling WORDS

1. store
2. or
3. door
4. more
5. corn
6. horse
7. floor
8. short
9. born
10. sort

YOUR OWN WORDS

Look for other words with the same vowel sound. Write them here.

11. Shone
12. poor

Each Spelling Word has the same vowel sound. Look at the letters—ore, or, or oor—that spell that sound. Write the Spelling Words in three groups to help you remember them.

core

store
more

torn

or
corn
horse
short
born
sort

Words with Two Vowels Together

floor
door

Words with the /ôr/ sound can be spelled ore, or, or oor.

Name Anthony

SPELLING CLUES: Spelling Rules Sometimes the same vowel sound can be spelled in different ways. Choose the spelling that looks correct. Then check the spelling.

Write the correct spelling of each Spelling Word.

1. mor (more) _more_   2. (corn) coorn _corn_

3. (sort) soort _sort_   4. boorn (born) _born_

5. dore (door) _door_   6. (short) shorte _short_

Write the correct spelling to tell about the pictures.
Then follow directions to color the pictures.

7. Color a blanket on the (horse, hoors). _horse_

8. Color a rug on the (flore, floor). _floor_

9. Color a window on the (stoor, store). _store_

Fun with Words Write a Spelling Word to tell about the pictures.

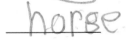

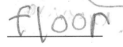

Which is more, 2 _or_ 4?

ALL KINDS OF FRIENDS "The Little Painter of Sabana Grande" • Harcourt Brace School Publishers

Name _____

Use Words to Explore to label the picture.
Then complete the sentence under the picture.

Words to Explore

artist
painting
colors
finished

The boy has _____ his picture. Do you like it?

What's in a Word?

Fernando lived in Panama. He painted pictures on the adobe walls of his house. Adobe is a Spanish word meaning "dried brick." Houses can be built of other things, too.

Write the word to tell what each house is made from.

brick   snow   straw   wood

_____   _____   _____   _____

ALL KINDS OF FRIENDS "The Little Painter of Sabana Grande" • Harcourt Brace School Publishers

Integrated Spelling

Name _____

CLASSIFYING Fernando painted many things on his house. Write each word in the correct group. Then add your own word to each group.

tree	toucan	sloth	vine
rooster	flower	monkey	leaves

_____   _____

PLANTS

ANIMALS

_____   _____

_____   _____

DICTIONARY Write these words in ABC order.

paint	brush	adobe	clay	Fernando

1. _____

2. _____

3. _____

4. _____

5. _____

WITH A PARTNER Draw a big house on a big piece of paper. On your house, paint pictures for five of the Spelling Words. Then label each picture with its Spelling Word.

Integrated Spelling   **Lesson 25   109**

ALL KINDS OF FRIENDS "The Little Painter of Sabana Grande" • Harcourt Brace School Publishers

Name _Anthony_

Words Like I've and won't

Spelling WORDS

1. don't
2. can't
3. let's
4. won't
5. I've
6. didn't
7. wasn't
8. couldn't
9. doesn't
10. wouldn't

YOUR OWN WORDS

Look for other contractions with _not_, _us_, and _have_. Write them here.

11. _clever_
12. _palace_

Each Spelling Word is a contraction. Look at the letters that spell each word.

Write the words in three groups to help you remember them.

not

don't
can't
won't
didn't
wasn't
couldn't
doesn't
wouldn't

have

I've

us

let's

Contractions can be made by combining words with _not_, _have_, and _us_.

Integrated Spelling

ALL KINDS OF FRIENDS "The Empty Pot" • Harcourt Brace School Publishers

Name Anthony

STRATEGY Workshop

SPELLING RULES: Contractions Think about the two words the contraction stands for. What letters are left out?

Write the Spelling Words that are the contractions for these words.

1. can   not   _can't_   2. could   not   _couldn't_

3. did   not   _didn't_   4. was   not   _wasn't_

Write the contractions that stand for the underlined words to complete these instructions for planting tulips.

Tulip Time

Let us _Let's_ plant some flowers.

I have _I've_ got tulip bulbs.

First, we'll dig a hole in the garden.

Next, we'll put in the bulb.

Last, we'll cover the bulb with dirt and then water it.

Remember: Do not _Don't_ add too much water.

Now we'll wait for spring.

Would not _wouldn't_ you like spring to come soon?

Fun with Words Complete each flower. Write the Spelling Word that stands for the two words.

will   not

does   not

ALL KINDS OF FRIENDS "The Empty Pot" • Harcourt Brace School Publishers

Integrated Spelling

VOCABULARY WordShop

Write Words to Explore to complete the sentences.

The emperor sat on his _throne_ in the ___palace___. He was looking for someone new to rule the country. Where could he find a _clever_ person who also had great _courage_?

Words to Explore

courage
clever
~~throne~~
~~palace~~

What's in a Word?

Emperor comes from a Latin word that means "to command." What does an emperor command? Some animals have <u>emperor</u> in their names.

Write each animal name to complete the sentence next to its picture.

| emperor goose | emperor of Japan | emperor butterfly | emperor penguin |

1. An _emperor penguin_ is the largest penguin.

2. The _emperor of Japan_ is a colorful fish.

3. The _emperor butterfly_ is a purple, spotted butterfly.

4. An _emperor goose_ is a large goose that lives near Alaska.

112 Lesson 26

Integrated Spelling

ALL KINDS OF FRIENDS "The Empty Pot" • Harcourt Brace School Publishers

Name _____

FLOWER WORDS Complete the time line by writing the word for each stage from seed to flower.

seed
flower
leaves
roots
buds
sprout

DESCRIBING WORDS Draw a picture of a flower you would like to grow. Then write four describing words to tell about your flower.

_____ _____

_____ _____

TRY THIS! Find the two words in each sentence that can be joined to make a Spelling Word. Circle the two words. Write the Spelling Word.

1. Ping could not grow a flower for the Emperor. _____

2. He watered the seed, but it would not grow. _____

3. "Let us see your flower," said the Emperor. _____

4. "I have tried," said Ping. _____

5. "But it did not grow." _____

6. "The seed will not grow," said the Emperor, "You told the truth. I make

   you Emperor of the land!" _____

Integrated Spelling

Lesson 26   113

ALL KINDS OF FRIENDS "The Empty Pot" • Harcourt Brace School Publishers

Name _Anthony_

Homophones

peasant
soldier

Spelling WORDS

1. so
2. to
3. for
4. there
5. sew
6. two
7. four
8. their
9. sow
10. too

YOUR OWN WORDS

Look for other words that are homophones. Write them here.

11. _____
12. _____

Homophones are words that sound alike but have different spellings and meanings. Say each Spelling Word aloud. Can you find the words that sound alike? Write the words in groups of homophones.

their
there

so
sow
sew

for
four

to
two
too

Homophones are words that sound alike but have different spellings and meanings.

ALL KINDS OF FRIENDS "Stone Soup" • Harcourt Brace School Publishers

STRATEGY Workshop

SPELLING CLUES: Homophones Think about the meaning you need. Choose one of the words. Spell the word. Then check the spelling. Write the correct Spelling Word to complete each sentence.

(their)   there   for   four

1. Will they share ___their___ soup?

2. I could eat ___four___ bowls of soup!

3. We can get some soup over ___there___.

4. That would be too much ___for___ me!

Use homophones to tell about the pictures. Write the correct spelling.

5. (sew, so) ___sew___ a skirt

6. (sew, sow) ___sow___ the seeds

7. (two, to) ___to___ the village

8. (too, two) ___two___ onions

Fun with Words Do word math. Write the Spelling Words you get.

9. os + t − o − t + o = ___so___

10. ot + s − o − s + o + o = ___too___

ALL KINDS OF FRIENDS "Stone Soup" • Harcourt Brace School Publishers

Name _____

VOCABULARY WordShop

Use Words to Explore to label the things in the kitchen.

Words to Explore

flavor

taste

supper

kettle

_____

_____

_____

Write a Word to Explore to complete the sentence.

The soup has a very good _____.

What's in a Word?

In the story "Stone Soup," the soldiers made soup in a big kettle. You can make soup, too.

Draw four ingredients in the soup kettle. Then label each ingredient you drew.

ALL KINDS OF FRIENDS "Stone Soup" • Harcourt Brace School Publishers

Integrated Spelling

ANTONYMS Complete the story by writing the opposite of each underlined word.

I love to eat <u>cold</u> _____ soup. I could eat it every <u>day</u> _____ for supper. The kind I like the <u>worst</u> _____ is vegetable soup. I think it tastes <u>awful</u> _____. I will make <u>none</u> _____ for you sometime!

DICTIONARY Write these soup ingredients in ABC order. Remember, if the first letters are the same, look at the second letters.

carrot   onion   ham   potato   celery

1.   2.   3.   4.   5.

ON YOUR OWN Choose two groups of homophones from the Spelling Words. Write sentences. Use all the homophones from a group in one sentence.

6. _____

7. _____

ALL KINDS OF FRIENDS "Stone Soup" • Harcourt Brace School Publishers

Name _____

Words That End with -ed and -ing

Spelling WORDS

1. asked
2. doing
3. called
4. going
5. looked
6. playing
7. started
8. trying
9. looking
10. wanted

YOUR OWN WORDS

Look for other words with the -ed or -ing ending. Write them here.

11. _____

12. _____

Each Spelling Word ends with -ed or -ing. Look at the letters that spell each ending.

Write the words in two groups to help you remember them.

walking
doing
going
playing
trying
looking

walked
asked
called
looked
started
wanted

Words can end with -ed or -ing.

ALL KINDS OF FRIENDS "The Night of the Stars" • Harcourt Brace School Publishers

Integrated Spelling

Name _____

STRATEGY Workshop

PROOFREADING: Check Spelling When you write, look at your spelling. Circle words you are unsure of. Then check the spelling.

Circle the word that is misspelled. Then write it correctly.

1. (goeing)   wanted   _going_   2. doing   (tring)   _trying_

3. (calld)   looked   _called_   4. (askd)   started   _asked_

Write the Spelling Words correctly to finish the story.

Starry Night

We wantd _wanted_ to see the shooting stars, so we went to the desert. We were warm in our sleeping bags as we lookt _looked_ at the dark sky. We were lookeing _looking_ very hard. Suddenly, the sky lit up. The stars were doeing _doing_ just what we had hoped. They were shooting through the sky.

Fun with Words Look at the picture puzzles.

Write a Spelling Word for each puzzle.

5. ⭐ + t + ed = _started_   6.  + ing = _playing_

ALL KINDS OF FRIENDS "The Night of the Stars" • Harcourt Brace School Publishers

VOCABULARY WordShop

Use a Word to Explore to complete each sentence.

Words
to Explore
· · · · · · · · · · · · ·
brilliant
light
disappear
glow

1. The _____ from the sun
   is fading.

2. The sky has a red _____.

3. The glow is _____.

4. The sun will _____ from sight.

What's in a Word?

The opposite of <u>sunset</u> is <u>sunrise</u>. The sun rises in the east and sets in the west. When the sun is right above your head, it is noon.

Draw pictures of the sun rising, the sun at noon, and the sun setting.
Label your pictures.

_____	_____	_____

ALL KINDS OF FRIENDS "The Night of the Stars" • Harcourt Brace School Publishers

Integrated Spelling

Name _____

COMPOUND WORDS Use the word <u>star</u> with these words to make compound words. Write each compound word under its picture.

| light | gazer | flower | fish | ship |

1. _____   2. _____   3. _____

4. _____   5. _____

ON YOUR OWN Write a Spelling Word for each tip of the star. Use the word shapes to help you.

6.

7.

8.

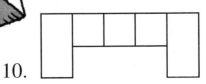

9.   10.

ALL KINDS OF FRIENDS "The Night of the Stars" • Harcourt Brace School Publishers

Integrated Spelling

Name _____

Practice Test

A. Read each sentence. Two words in each sentence are underlined. Find the word that is spelled correctly. Mark the letter for that word.

1. I like to read about places that <u>are</u> <u>fer</u> from home.
          A   B

   1. Ⓐ Ⓑ

2. I <u>cant</u> wait to visit a <u>farm</u>.
     A   B

   2. Ⓐ Ⓑ

3. Bad weather makes it <u>hard</u> to grow <u>corne</u>.
        A   B

   3. Ⓐ Ⓑ

4. I'm planting <u>four</u> rows of beets in the <u>parke</u>.
       A   B

   4. Ⓐ Ⓑ

5. I <u>started</u> telling my friends <u>too</u> water the buds.
      A   B

   5. Ⓐ Ⓑ

6. <u>Won't</u> it be fun to <u>sorte</u> all the vegetables?
     A   B

   6. Ⓐ Ⓑ

7. Everyone <u>asked</u> me to plant lots <u>moor</u>.
        A   B

   7. Ⓐ Ⓑ

ALL KINDS OF FRIENDS Unit 2 Review • Harcourt Brace School Publishers

Integrated Spelling

Name _____

B. Read each sentence. Two words in each sentence are underlined. Find the word that is spelled correctly. Mark the letter for that word.

1. It <u>looked</u> as if <u>their</u> might be a frost.
        A   B

2. I'm <u>going</u> to <u>so</u> cloth to cover the sprouts.
           A   B

3. <u>Iv'e</u> always <u>wanted</u> to have a garden.
     A   B

4. You can <u>stour</u> vegetables <u>for</u> the winter.
           A   B

5. The cellar <u>floor</u> is cold and <u>deark</u>.
          A   B

6. This fall I'm <u>doeing</u> some canning, <u>too</u>.
            A   B

7. <u>Let's</u> eat tomato relish <u>ore</u> pickles.
     A   B

8. <u>Wouldn't</u> you like to <u>stert</u> eating now?
       A   B

1. Ⓐ Ⓑ
2. Ⓐ Ⓑ
3. Ⓐ Ⓑ
4. Ⓐ Ⓑ
5. Ⓐ Ⓑ
6. Ⓐ Ⓑ
7. Ⓐ Ⓑ
8. Ⓐ Ⓑ

ALL KINDS OF FRIENDS Unit 2 Review • Harcourt Brace School Publishers

Name _____

SPIN THE GLOBE

Words to Watch For

children
from
now
their
today

Read a book about another country. It can be a story or a myth or a fairy tale. It can be a nonfiction book. As you are reading, take some notes. Then, after you have finished the book, write a book report. Make sure you include the names of the book, the author, and the illustrator. Tell something about what happens in the book or what kinds of information it gives. Last, tell why you liked or didn't like the book. Use this space to write down the countries you might want to read about.

TIPS FOR SPELLING SUCCESS Be sure to use capital letters when you write the title of your book and the names of the author and the illustrator. Read your finished book report to check for spelling errors.

ALL KINDS OF FRIENDS Unit 2 Review • Harcourt Brace School Publishers

Integrated Spelling

PLAYTIME

Think about the many toys, games, and hobbies you have read about in class. Suppose you were an inventor. What toy, game, or hobby would you create? Would it be something for indoors or outdoors? Would it have a game board? Would it be small enough to put in a suitcase or so very large that it has to stay in your room? Draw a picture of your toy, game, or hobby. Then write a set of directions telling how to use it.

TIPS FOR SPELLING SUCCESS Check to see that your directions are clear and easy to understand. Read them again and look for spelling errors.

WORD DOODLES

Use the clues to finish the rhymes. Add two letters.

Slam the __d__ __ __ __ __r__ .

Mop the __f__ __l__ __ __ __ __r__ .

Do you hear the __l__ __ __ __ __k__

Singing in the __p__ __ __ __ __k__ ?

TIPS FOR SPELLING SUCCESS Use what you know about the letter combinations that spell vowel sounds to help you write new words.

ALL KINDS OF FRIENDS Unit 2 Review • Harcourt Brace School Publishers

Name _Anthony_

Words to Remember

Spelling WORDS

1. about
2. down
3. after
4. how
5. because
6. out
7. other
8. were
9. very
10. over

YOUR OWN WORDS

Look for other words that you use often. Write them here.

11.  brother
12. sister

Each Spelling Word is a word that you use often. Look at the letters that spell those words.

Write the words in groups to help you remember them.

ou
about
out

er
after
other
were
very
over
brother
sister

ow
down
how

be
because

Some words are used often. Think about how these words are spelled.

ALL KINDS OF FRIENDS "The Goat in the Rug" • Harcourt Brace School Publishers

Name _____

STRATEGY Workshop

PROOFREADING: Check Spelling After you write, look for words that look wrong. Circle the words. Check the spelling.

Circle the word that is misspelled. Write that Spelling Word correctly.

1. (wer) over _were_

2. (aftere) down _after_

3. about (othre) _other_

4. (owt) very _out_

Circle each word that is misspelled. Write that Spelling Word correctly.

The family downe _down_ the street from me has a goat. It is abowte _about_ one year old. It must be a vere _very_ hungry goat becawse _because_ it eats everything! I wonder houe _how_ much it can eat in one day!

Fun with Words Use a Spelling Word to tell about the picture.

Hey diddle, diddle,
    the cat and the fiddle,
The goat jumped _over_
    the moon.

ALL KINDS OF FRIENDS "The Goat in the Rug" • Harcourt Brace School Publishers

Name Anthony

VOCABULARY WordShop

Use a Word to Explore to tell about each picture.

Words
to Explore
....
design
weave
wool
loom

1. Will you __weave__ a rug for me?

2. Draw a picture of the __design__ you want.

3. We'll use this __wool__ from one of our sheep.

4. Use a __loom__ to weave the yarn into a rug!

What's in a Word?

You can <u>weave</u> yarn into a rug. You can also <u>weave your way</u> somewhere by turning or twisting as you go.

Weave your way through this maze. Can you find the loom?

ALL KINDS OF FRIENDS "The Goat in the Rug" • Harcourt Brace School Publishers

Integrated Spelling

Name _____

CLASSIFYING Rugs can be made from wool. What else might you make from wool? What might you make from wood? Write each word around the correct picture. Then add words of your own.

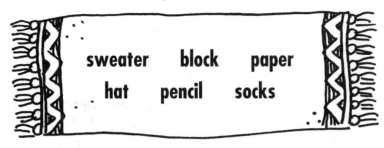

sweater   block   paper

hat   pencil   socks

_____   _____

   _____   _____   

_____   _____

DICTIONARY Put the words in ABC order to write a sentence. Remember the period (.) at the end.

likes	Ed	yarn	wool	to	with	weave

1. _____

TRY THIS! Write the Spelling Word that means the opposite of each word.

2. before _____

3. in _____

4. up _____

5. under _____

ALL KINDS OF FRIENDS "The Goat in the Rug" • Harcourt Brace School Publishers

Name Anthony

Compound Words

1. upon
2. grandma
3. seesaw
4. sometimes
5. herself
6. somewhere
7. classroom
8. himself
9. baseball
10. something

YOUR OWN WORDS

Look for other compound words. Write them here.

11. lunchtime
12. butterfly

Each Spelling Word is a compound word. Look for the two smaller words in each Spelling Word.

Write the Spelling Words in a way that will help you remember them.

self
himself
herself

some
sometimes
something
somewhere

Other Compound Words
upon   classroom
grandma   baseball
seesaw   lunchtime

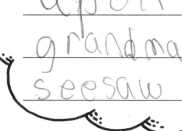
A compound word is a word made from two smaller words.

ALL KINDS OF FRIENDS "Thunder Cake" • Harcourt Brace School Publishers

Name Anthony

STRATEGY Workshop

SPELLING CLUES: Compound Words How do you spell the smaller words in a compound word? Write them together. Does the spelling look correct?

Combine the words to make a compound word. Write the Spelling Words.

1. see + saw _____Seesaw_____
2. base + ball _____baseball_____
3. class + room _____classroom_____
4. him + self _____himself_____

Combine the words to make compound words.
Write the Spelling Words.

A Lifelong Cook

Some + times _____sometimes_____ get very hungry, especially after school. That's when I make some + thing _____something_____ delicious to eat. My grand + ma _____grandma_____ helps me. She is a great cook. She will tell you that her + self _____heself_____. After all, she has been practicing for a long time!

Fun with Words Make two Spelling Words.
Write them in the puddles.

upon

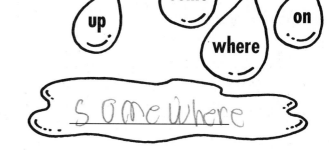

somewhere

ALL KINDS OF FRIENDS "Thunder Cake" • Harcourt Brace School Publishers

Name _____

VOCABULARY WordShop

Use a Word to Explore to complete each sentence.

Words to Explore

distance

lightning

storm

weather

1. I love rainy _____.

2. Do you see that flash of _____?

3. I can hear thunder in the _____.

4. This is a real _____.

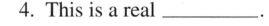

What's in a Word?

In the story "Thunder Cake," Grandma always made a thunder cake before a thunderstorm arrived.

Make up your own names for these foods.

5. cookies you always eat when there's lightning

_____

6. soup you always cook on a rainy day

_____

7. salad you eat every Sunday

_____

8. sandwich you make on the first day of spring

_____

132   Lesson 31

Integrated Spelling

ALL KINDS OF FRIENDS "Thunder Cake" • Harcourt Brace School Publishers

Name _____

DESCRIBING WORDS The girl in the story "Thunder Cake" was brave. Write words that describe the people in the pictures.

| angry | happy | scared | tired | sad | surprised |

1. _____

2. _____

3. _____

4. _____

5. _____

6. _____

COMPOUND WORDS Rewrite each sentence. Use a compound word in place of the underlined words.

7. Did you find the room with the class?

_____

8. I got the ball to use in the game with a base.

_____

WITH A PARTNER Write each Spelling Word on a card. Then cut each Spelling Word between the two smaller words. Turn all the cards over. Play a memory game. Match the words to make Spelling Words.

Integrated Spelling

ALL KINDS OF FRIENDS "Thunder Cake" • Harcourt Brace School Publishers

Words Like dropped and running

Spelling WORDS

1. dropped
2. putting
3. stopped
4. getting
5. planned
6. running
7. slipped
8. sitting
9. grabbed
10. popping

YOUR OWN WORDS

Look for other words with a double final consonant before -ed or -ing. Write them here.

11. _____
12. _____

Each Spelling Word ends with -ed or -ing. Look at the letters that spell those endings. The final consonant was doubled before the ending was added.

Write the words in two groups to help you remember them.

hopping

hopped

In some words you must double the final consonant before adding -ed or -ing.

Integrated Spelling

ALL KINDS OF FRIENDS "Ant Cities" • Harcourt Brace School Publishers

Name _____

STRATEGY Workshop

SPELLING CLUES: Spelling Rules Think about the rule for doubling the final consonant. Try spelling the word. Does it look right?

Add the ending to each word. Remember to double the final consonant. Write the Spelling Word.

1. drop (**ed**) _____

2. grab (**ed**) _____

3. put (**ing**) _____

4. stop (**ed**) _____

Add the ending to each underlined word to tell about the ant fair. Write the Spelling Word.

Under the Magnifying Glass

There's a fair going on at Anthill. Balloons are pop(ing) _____. One ant is get(ing) _____ on the merry-go-round. Another is sit(ing) _____ on the Ferris wheel. The ants have plan(ed) _____ a great day!

Fun with Words Unscramble the letters to write a Spelling Word that tells about each picture.

n n r u i n g

5. _____

e d i p p s l

6. _____

ALL KINDS OF FRIENDS "Ant Cities" • Harcourt Brace School Publishers

VOCABULARY WordShop

Use Words to Explore to tell about the picture.

Words
to Explore
....
built

tunnel

carried

dug

1. The ants _____ a nest.

2. They _____ a long _____.

3. Some ants _____ in food.

What's in a Word?

A carpenter is someone who builds with wood. Carpenter ants build their nests in wood.

4. Pavement is another name for a sidewalk. Where do you think pavement

   ants live? _____

5. What do you think leaf-cutting ants make their nests with?

   _____

ALL KINDS OF FRIENDS "Ant Cities" • Harcourt Brace School Publishers

Name _____

ACTION WORDS Write the word that tells what each ant is doing.

| run eat dig climb ride sit |

1. _____   2. _____   3. _____

4. _____   5. _____   6. _____

DICTIONARY Write the words in ABC order.

| ant nest carpenter anthill carry |

_____ _____ _____ _____ _____

ON YOUR OWN Draw five ants. In each body part of each ant, write part of a Spelling Word. Put the base word in the first part, the doubled consonant in the middle, and the ending in the last part.

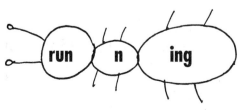

Integrated Spelling

ALL KINDS OF FRIENDS "Ant Cities" • Harcourt Brace School Publishers

Name _____

Words Like loved and moving

1. _saved_
2. _giving_
3. _liked_
4. _taking_
5. _used_
6. _riding_
7. _placed_
8. _moving_
9. _loved_
10. _living_

YOUR OWN WORDS

Look for other words where the final _e_ was dropped before -ed or -ing was added. Write them here.

11. _____
12. _____

Each Spelling Word ends with -ed or -ing. Look at the letters that spell those endings. The final _e_ was dropped before the ending was added.

  Write the words in two groups to help you remember them.

skated   **skating**

_____   _____

_____   _____

_____   _____

_____   _____

_____   _____

In some words, you must drop the final _e_ before adding -ed or -ing.

ALL KINDS OF FRIENDS "Ibis: A True Whale Story" • Harcourt Brace School Publishers

Integrated Spelling

Name _____

STRATEGY Workshop

SPELLING CLUES: Spelling Rules Think about the rule for dropping final <u>e</u>. Try spelling the word. Does it look right?

Add the ending to each word. Remember to drop the final <u>e</u>. Write the Spelling Word.

1. give (ing) _____

2. place (ed) _____

3. like (ed) _____

4. live (ing) _____

Finish the story. Add the ending to each word. Then write the Spelling Word.

A Whale of a Dream

I had a dream last night! A whale was

move (ing) _____ through the water. I

was ride (ing) _____ on its back! It was

take (ing) _____ me for quite a ride!

I love (ed) _____ flying through the

water. I hated waking up from my dream!

Fun with Words Write the Spelling Words that fit in each shape to complete the sentences.

5. The whale _____ its baby.

6. It _____ its nose to push the baby up for air.

ALL KINDS OF FRIENDS "Ibis: A True Whale Story" • Harcourt Brace School Publishers

Name _____

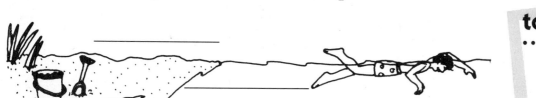

Use Words to Explore to tell about the picture.

Words to Explore

coast

surface

tangled

whale

A whale is a large sea mammal. A whale of a time means "a very wonderful or big time."

Make up some of your own whale of a phrases to describe wonderful things you have done.

ALL KINDS OF FRIENDS "Ibis: A True Whale Story" • Harcourt Brace School Publishers

Integrated Spelling

Name _____

SYNONYMS Do the crossword puzzle. Write a word that means almost the same as each underlined word.

| smart | large | tired | small | fast |

Across

2. A whale is not <u>little</u>.

4. Do you think whales get <u>sleepy</u>?

Down

1. Are whales <u>quick</u> swimmers?

2. Whales are <u>intelligent</u>.

3. A blue whale is really <u>big</u>!

WITH A PARTNER Play a game. Write a blank for each letter in a Spelling Word. As your partner chooses letters, write them where they go in the word or to the side. Take turns. Spell all the words!

m _ v i _ g

ALL KINDS OF FRIENDS "Ibis: A True Whale Story" • Harcourt Brace School Publishers

Name _____

Plurals

Spelling WORDS

1. girls
2. boxes
3. toys
4. dishes
5. times
6. inches
7. boys
8. wishes
9. days
10. things

YOUR OWN WORDS

Look for other words that are plurals. Write them here.

11. _____

12. _____

Each Spelling Word is a plural, or means "more than one." Look at the letter or letters, <u>s</u> or <u>es</u>, that were added to make the plurals.

Write the words in two groups to help you remember them.

s

girls
toys
boys
days
things

es

boxes
dishes
times
inches
wishes

You can make plurals by adding -<u>s</u> or -<u>es</u>.

ALL KINDS OF FRIENDS "Sam the Sea Cow" • Harcourt Brace School Publishers

Integrated Spelling

Name _____

STRATEGY Workshop

SPELLING CLUES: Spelling Rules Think about the rules for adding -s and -es to words. Then spell the word. Does it look right?

Add -s or -es to each word to make it mean "more than one." Then write the Spelling Word.

1. inch_es_ _inches_

2. toy__ _____

3. time_s_ _times_

4. dish__ _____

Add -s or -es to make plurals. Then write the Spelling Words.

It is Sam's birthday and he makes some (wish) _____. He wants many (thing) _____, but they don't come in (box) _____! He wants clean and safe water for sea cows to swim in all the (day) _____ of their lives.

Fun with Words Write Spelling Words to finish the sentence.

5. The _____ and _____ watch the sea cow swim.

ALL KINDS OF FRIENDS "Sam the Sea Cow" • Harcourt Brace School Publishers

Name _____

VOCABULARY WordShop

Use Words to Explore to tell about the picture.

Words to Explore

noise

explore

finally

harmless

This manatee will _____ everything it sees. The herons are

_____ friends. Do you think the manatee can see their feet? Can

the manatee hear any _____? The manatee _____ heads home

for a nap.

SEA MAMMALS The manatee is a sea mammal. Write the names of these other

mammals under their pictures.

walrus   dolphin   whale

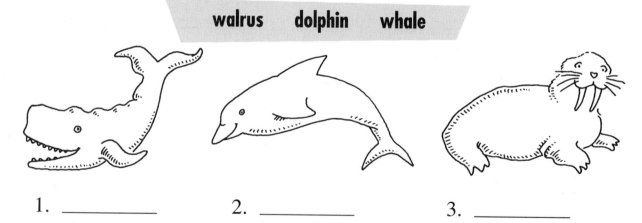

1. _____   2. _____   3. _____

4. Now draw a picture of a land
   mammal. Label your picture.

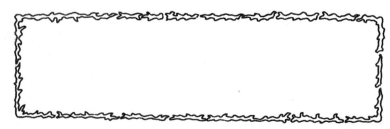

_____

ALL KINDS OF FRIENDS "Sam the Sea Cow" • Harcourt Brace School Publishers

Name _____

What's in a Word?

Is a <u>sea cow</u> a cow that lives in the sea? No—it's another name for a manatee.

Look at these pictures. Complete the sentences to find out about some other "sea" animals.

| walrus | hippopotamus | porpoise | dogfish |

1. A sea cow can also be a _____.

2. This _____ is sometimes called a sea dog.

3. A _____ is sometimes called a sea hog.

4. A _____ is sometimes called a sea horse.

ON YOUR OWN Answer each riddle with a Spelling Word. Then choose three other Spelling Words. Write riddles for them. Tell your riddles to a classmate.

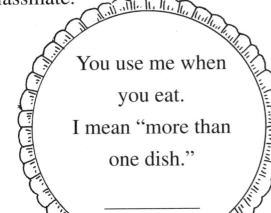

You use me when you eat.
I mean "more than one dish."

_____

You put things in me.
I mean "more than one box."

_____

ALL KINDS OF FRIENDS "Sam the Sea Cow" • Harcourt Brace School Publishers

UNIT REVIEW

Name _____

Practice Test

A. Read each word list. Choose the correctly spelled word that fits in the blank. Mark the letter next to that word.

1. fall _____
   - Ⓐ down
   - Ⓑ donw
   - Ⓒ downe

2. balloons _____
   - Ⓐ poping
   - Ⓑ popping
   - Ⓒ popeing

3. visit _____
   - Ⓐ grandmae
   - Ⓑ grandma
   - Ⓒ granma

4. moving _____
   - Ⓐ oute
   - Ⓑ owt
   - Ⓒ out

5. toy _____
   - Ⓐ boxs
   - Ⓑ boxis
   - Ⓒ boxes

6. once _____ a time
   - Ⓐ upon
   - Ⓑ unpo
   - Ⓒ upone

7. going _____
   - Ⓐ riding
   - Ⓑ rideing
   - Ⓒ ridding

8. three _____
   - Ⓐ wishs
   - Ⓑ wishes
   - Ⓒ wises

ALL KINDS OF FRIENDS Unit 3 Review • Harcourt Brace School Publishers

Integrated Spelling

Name Bailey / LOL

B. Look at the three spelling choices for each word. Choose the correct one. Mark the letter for that word.

1. (A) because
   (B) becuse
   (C) becaus

2. (A) giving
   (B) giveing
   (C) givving

3. (A) basball
   (B) basebal
   (C) baseball

4. (A) after
   (B) atfer
   (C) aftr

5. (A) dishs
   (B) diches
   (C) dishes

6. (A) somewere
   (B) somwhere
   (C) somewhere

7. (A) stoped
   (B) stopped
   (C) stoppd

8. (A) inchs
   (B) inches
   (C) inchis

ALL KINDS OF FRIENDS Unit 3 Review • Harcourt Brace School Publishers

Name _____

HELPING THE EARTH

Words
to Watch For

brought

can

don't

friend

good

tomorrow

Think of a recycling project for your class. Make a list of the many things you can recycle. Choose the ones that are best for your class to collect. Then decide where and when you will do your recycling. Next, make a poster to tell people about your project. Write down all the important facts: what, when, and where. Draw a picture. Finally, write a slogan or a few sentences that will convince people to help you with your project. Use this space to work out some project ideas.

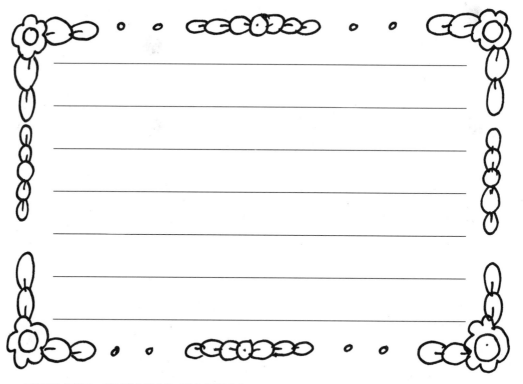

TIPS FOR SPELLING SUCCESS Make sure that you use -er and -est words correctly. Check to see that the information on your poster is clear and that there are no spelling errors.

ALL KINDS OF FRIENDS Unit 3 Review • Harcourt Brace School Publishers

Integrated Spelling

MEDAL WINNER

Think about how the people and animals in the stories you have read helped each other. Choose your favorite person or animal. Then make a medal for that person or animal. Write a short speech to give when you present the medal. Display your medal in the classroom.

TIPS FOR SPELLING SUCCESS Begin each name with a capital letter. Read your speech to look for spelling errors.

WORD DOODLES

Use the clues to help you do the picture puzzles.

1. Add an -s or an -es.

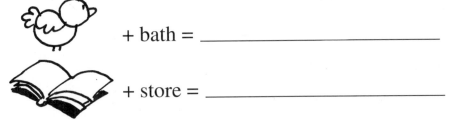

2. Write a word to make a compound word.

    + bath = _____

    + store = _____

TIPS FOR SPELLING SUCCESS Use what you know about the ways to form plurals when you write a new word. Use what you know about the two small words when you write a compound word.

ALL KINDS OF FRIENDS Unit 3 Review • Harcourt Brace School Publishers

SPELLING DICTIONARY

Here is your Spelling Dictionary! You will find all your Spelling Words and Words to Explore in it.

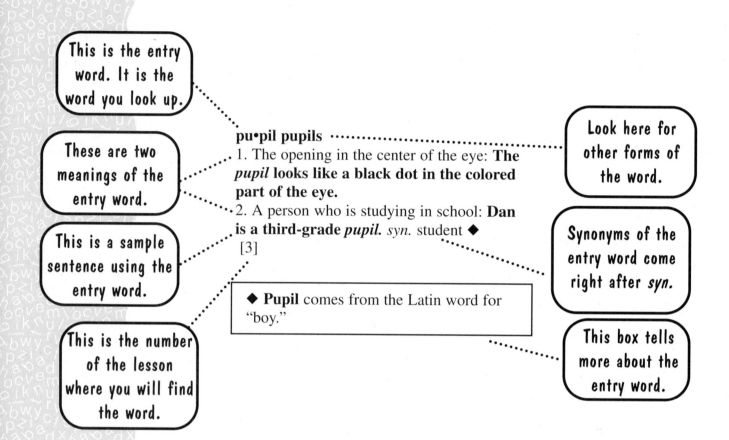

This is the entry word. It is the word you look up.

These are two meanings of the entry word.

This is a sample sentence using the entry word.

This is the number of the lesson where you will find the word.

pu•pil pupils
1. The opening in the center of the eye: **The** *pupil* **looks like a black dot in the colored part of the eye.**
2. A person who is studying in school: **Dan is a third-grade** *pupil.* *syn.* student ◆
[3]

◆ **Pupil** comes from the Latin word for "boy."

Look here for other forms of the word.

Synonyms of the entry word come right after *syn.*

This box tells more about the entry word.

Spelling Table

The Spelling Table below has the sounds that we use to speak the words of English. The first column of the table gives the pronunciation symbol for the sound, such as ō. The second column of the table gives an example of a common word in which this sound appears, such as **open** for the /ō/ sound. The third column of the table provides examples of the different ways that the sound can be spelled, such as as **oh, o, oa, ow,** and **oe** for the /ō/ sound.

The Sound	In	Is Spelled As	The Sound	In	Is Spelled As
a	add	cat	ng	ring	thing
ā	age	game, rain, day, steak, weigh	o	odd	pot
ä	palm	ah, father, dark, heart	ō	open	oh, over, go, oak, grow, toe
â(r)	care	dare, fair, where, bear, their	ô	order	for, more, roar, ball, walk, dawn, fault, ought
b	bat	big, cabin	oi	oil	noise, toy
ch	check	chop, march, catch	o͝o	took	foot, would
d	dog	dig, bad	o͞o	pool	cool, soup, through, rude, due, fruit, drew
e	end	egg, met, ready			
ē	equal	she, eat, see, key, field, receive, city, here, dear, steer	ou	out	ounce, now
			p	put	pin, cap
			r	run	red, car, wrist
f	fit	five, offer, cough, photo	s	see	sit, scene, loss, city
g	go	gate, ghost	sh	rush	shoe, ocean, special
h	hot	hope, who	t	top	tan, kept
i	it	inch, hit	th	thin	think, cloth
ī	ice	item, fine, pie, high, try	th	this	these, clothing
j	joy	jump, gem, magic, cage, edge	u	up	cut, butter, flood, young
			û(r)	burn	turn, bird, work, early, herd
k	keep	king, cat, lock, chorus, account	v	very	vote, over
			w	win	wait, towel
l	look	let, ball	y	yet	year
m	move	make, climb	yo͞o	use	cue, few
n	nice	new, can, know, gnome	z	zoo	zebra, lazy, buzz

A

a•bout **1.** being near a certain amount; almost: **It is** *about* **one mile from our house to my school. 2.** having something to do with: **Charlotte's Web is a book** *about* **animals on a farm.** [30]

a•bove in a higher place; over: **There was a sign** *above* **the door that said "EXIT."** [10]

add **1.** to put one thing with another; combine: **Put the soup in the pot, and** *add* **one can of water. 2.** to put numbers together: **When you** *add* **the numbers 4 and 6, you get 10.** [15]

ad•ven•ture something that is exciting or unusual: **Going across the ocean from England to America was a real** *adventure* **in the days of sailing ships.** [10]

af•ter **1.** at a later time; after now: **June is the month that comes** *after* **May. 2.** along with and behind: **Tim went out the door, and his dog ran** *after* **him.** [30]

a•gainst **1.** in the other direction; opposite: **Our team played a softball game** *against* **the Redbirds. 2.** so as to touch; in contact with: **She leaned her bicycle** *against* **the wall.** [22]

all every one of something; the whole thing: *All* **fish live in water.** [15]

an a special word used before a noun or adjective that begins with the sound of *a, e, i, o,* or *u*: **I had** *an* **apple for lunch, and she had** *an* **orange.** *An* **elephant is** *an* **enormous animal.** [1] ♦

♦ **An, a,** and **the** are special words called *articles.* We use articles to point out a certain thing. **An** goes before a word with a *vowel sound* (a, e, i, o, u).

---

an•gry very mad: **The man was** *angry*

when he spilled grape juice all over his new white rug. [18]

are a special word used when talking about more than one person or thing: **These shoes** *are* **new. Karen and Rosa** *are* **friends of mine.** [24]

arm **1.** the part of the body between the shoulder and the hand: **Keesha's** *arm* **was tired after she pitched in the baseball game. 2.** something that looks or works like an arm: **The cat was sleeping on the** *arm* **of the chair.** [24]

ar•tist a person who draws or paints: **A person who paints pictures is an** *artist.* [25]

asked used words to try to find out something: **I didn't hear the teacher, so I** *asked* **my friend what she said.** [28]

a•void to stay away from: **That road always has a lot of traffic, so we** *avoid* **it and take another road.** [22]

aw•ful very bad: **There was an** *awful* **flood and many people had to leave their homes.** [18]

B

bad **1.** not good; not as is wanted or as it should be: **He had only two answers right, so he got a** *bad* **score on the test. 2.** causing a problem or difficulty: **She was sick in bed with a** *bad* **cold.** [1]

ball **1.** a round object: **The cat plays with a** *ball* **of yarn. 2.** a thing with a round shape that is used to play certain games: **In soccer you try to kick the** *ball* **into the goal.** [15]

bal•loon a small rubber bag filled with air: **On my birthday, I got a big red** *balloon* **that said "Happy Birthday."** [16]

base•ball   **1.** a game that is played on a field in which one team tries to hit the ball and run around the bases to score a run. The other team tries to catch the ball to get the runners out: *Baseball* **is a popular game in the United States. 2.** the ball that is used in this game: **A** *baseball* **is hard, and players wear gloves when they try to catch it.** [31]

bat   **1.** a long stick that is made of wood or metal, used to hit a baseball: **A wooden** *bat* **makes a loud cracking sound when it hits the ball. 2.** a small mouselike animal that has wings made of very thin skin: **A** *bat* **sleeps during the day and flies at night.** [1]

bath   a washing of the body with water: **He takes a** *bath* **every night before he goes to bed.** [18]

bath

be•cause   for the reason that: **I woke up late** *because* **my alarm clock did not go off.** [30]

be•gan   set off to do something; started: **She** *began* **her speech by saying, "Good morning, everyone."** [2]

bet   to feel strongly that something will happen: **The sky looks really dark. I** *bet* **it will rain today.** [2]

bike   a shorter word for **bicycle,** a vehicle with two wheels that people ride on: **I ride my** *bike* **to school every day.** [2]

bit   **1.** a very small amount: **He couldn't hear the radio, so he turned up the sound a** *bit.* **2.** something very small:

She tore up the paper into tiny *bits.* **3.** grabbed or cut with the teeth: **Tara** *bit* **into the apple.** [3]

black   a color that is the opposite of white; the darkest color: **A killer whale is** *black* **with white markings.** [19]

blow   to send air out strongly, as from the mouth: **You will have to** *blow* **very hard to put out all the candles.** [14]

boat   a thing that floats on water and moves by means of oars, sails, or an engine: **Jason likes to sail his toy** *boat* **on the pond.** ♦ [10]

───────────────────

♦ **Boat** and **ship** are two words that are close in meaning. Boats and ships both carry people on the water. A boat is small and carries a few people, usually for a short distance. A ship is much larger and can carry many people across an ocean.

───────────────────

bone   one of the hard white parts that make up the skeleton of a person's or animal's body: **Cory broke a** *bone* **in his arm.** [13]

book   a set of pages with words printed on them, held together inside a cover: **A dictionary is a** *book* **that tells how to spell words and what they mean.** [19]

bor•ing   not interesting; not fun: **They thought the movie was** *boring,* **so they left the theater before it was over.** [20]

born   brought into life: **My grandmother was** *born* **in 1928.** [25]

both   the two together: <u>Here</u> **and** <u>hear</u> **are different words, but they** *both* **have the same sound.** [7]

box   a container that is used to hold things: **When we got our new computer home, we had to take it out of the** *box.* **Some kinds of food are sold in** *boxes,* **such as cereal, crackers, and candy.** [4, 34]

boys   male children; children who are not girls: **There are twelve *boys* and fifteen girls in my class at school.** [34]

brave   facing danger with courage: **The *brave* woman jumped into the water to save a baby.** [2]

bright   **1.** giving off much light; shining with a strong light: **She had to put on her sunglasses because the sun was very *bright*. 2.** having a good mind; smart: **Maria is a *bright* child who gets A's in all her subjects.** [22]

bril•liant   **1.** very bright; glowing: **The diamond sparkled with a *brilliant* light. 2.** having a very good mind; very smart: **Dr. Seuss was a *brilliant* writer who wrote some of the world's funniest books for children.** [28]

brought   took along from one place to another: **She thought it might rain, so she *brought* an umbrella with her.** [16]

built   made something; put something together: **Some American pioneers lived in cabins that they *built* with logs.** [32]

bur•row   **1.** a hole made in the ground by an animal: **A mole lives in a *burrow*. 2.** to make a hole in the ground: **The mole can *burrow* for many feet underground.** [19]

bus   a large motor vehicle with many rows of seats for carrying a large number of people: **The school *bus* stops at our corner at 7:45 each morning. ♦** [6]

♦ **Bus** comes from the word **omnibus.** The word *omni* means "all." The idea is that a bus is for all people. A car is owned by one person or family, but anyone can pay to ride on a bus.

---

by   **1.** by means of; through: **They sent the package *by* mail. 2.** next to; near: **Mom told us to wait for her *by* the door. 3.** not later than: **Our book reports have to be finished *by* Friday.** [7]

call   to talk to a person on the telephone: **I'm going to *call* Kevin to find out if he can play later.** [15]

called   said something in a loud voice: **I *called* to my friend when I saw him across the street.** [28]

can't   cannot; is not able to: **My brother is only three, and he *can't* read yet.** [26]

car   a four-wheeled motor vehicle that carries people: **A *car* is also called an "automobile."** [19]

care   **1.** to look after; watch over: **A mother bear will *care* for her cubs until they are about two years old. 2.** to have feelings for or about: **It rained at our picnic, but I didn't *care* because we had fun anyway.** [19]

car•ried   held and taken from one place to another: **He *carried* his books to school in his backpack.** [32]

cat   a small furry animal with pointed ears, sharp claws, and a long tail, often kept as a pet: **A *cat* makes a fine indoor pet.** [1]

cat

caught   **1.** got, became infected: **Maria Elena *caught* a cold at camp. 2.** took hold of something moving: **He reached up and *caught* the ball in his hand.** [12]

cel•e•brate   to have a good time or do certain things because of a special time: **People like to *celebrate* Thanksgiving by getting the whole family together for a big dinner.** [15]

change 1. to make or become different: **I asked the teacher to *change* my seat so that I would be closer to the board.** 2. money given back when a person pays more than something costs: **She gave the clerk one dollar for a fruit drink that cost 75 cents and got 25 cents in *change*.** [16, 21]

chest 1. a box with a lid attached, used to store things: **Billy put his blocks into the toy *chest*.** 2. the part of the body where the heart is: **The *chest* is between the shoulders and the waist.** [16]

child 1. a young boy or girl: **When my mother was a *child*, she lived on a farm.** 2. someone's son or daughter: **Abraham Lincoln was the *child* of a poor Kentucky farmer.** [7]

class•room a room in a school where classes are held: **Our *classroom* has pictures of animals on the walls.** [31]

clev•er smart; good at doing things: **Our coach had a *clever* idea for what we could do to win the game.** [26]

coal a black material that is dug out of the ground and used for fuel: **When *coal* is burned in a furnace, it gives off a great amount of heat.** [10]

coast 1. the land at the edge of a sea or ocean: **San Francisco is a city on the Pacific *coast*.** 2. to ride on a bicycle or in a car without using power: **He took his feet off the pedals so that he could *coast* down the hill.** [10, 33]

coat 1. a piece of clothing with sleeves, worn over other clothes to keep warm: **In winter, I wear a wool *coat* almost every day.** 2. the hair or fur of an animal: **Our pet bunny has a very soft *coat*.** 3. a thin layer or covering: **The outside of our house needs a new *coat* of paint.** [10]

cold 1. having a very low temperature; not hot: **It sometimes snows when the weather is very *cold*.** 2. an illness with sneezing, coughing, and a runny nose: **I stayed home from school yesterday because I had a *cold*.** [7] ◆

◆ **Cold** might seem to be the wrong name for a kind of sickness. When you are sick with this, you often feel hot, not cold. The name comes from the idea that people get colds more often in the winter. This is the time of the year when it is cold.

---

col•or the different ways we see the light from something; red, blue, yellow, and so on: **My favorite *colors* are purple and blue.** [25]

com•pa•ny 1. someone who comes to visit; a guest or guests: **We're having *company* for dinner tonight.** 2. a group of people who work together; a business: **That *company* sells computers.** [7]

cook•ies small, sweet cakes that are usually flat and round: **He had a snack of milk and oatmeal *cookies*.** [6]

corn a kind of tall plant that is often eaten as a vegetable: **The parts of *corn* that we eat are the kernels, which are usually yellow or white.** [25]

cough a rough sound made by sending air out through the mouth from the chest: **My baby sister has a *cough*.** [12]

could•n't could not; was or were not able to: **We kept playing until it got so dark that we *couldn't* see the ball.** [26]

cour•age bravery when facing something dangerous or when afraid: **A firefighter has to have *courage* to enter a burning building.** [26]

co•zy warm and comfortable: **The dog found a *cozy* spot near the fireplace and went to sleep.** [19]

cry to have tears coming out from the eyes: **The movie about the lost little dog made Abby so sad that she began to *cry*.** [22]

cup a small round container used for drinking: **People often drink hot chocolate from a *cup*.** [6]

cup

cut **1.** to make an opening in something using a sharp tool: **She used a knife to *cut* the piece of string. 2.** to be hurt by something sharp going through the skin: **Marty *cut* his foot when he stepped on some broken glass.** [6]

cute nice to look at; pretty: **Our dog was so *cute* when she was a puppy.** [13] ◆

◆ **Cute** is usually used to talk about something that is small and young: **That is a very *cute* picture of the baby because of the smile on his face.**

dad a friendly name for a father: **My *dad* said I did a good job on my book report.** [1]

dark having little or no light: **He turned off the TV, and the screen was *dark*.** [24]

days the time when the sun is out; the time that is not night: **Many people work or go to school five *days* each week.** [34]

de•cide to make up one's mind what to do: **I like both shirts, and I just can't *decide* which one to wear.** [13]

deep going far down from the top or the surface: **The water is very *deep* in the middle of the ocean.** [9]

de•li•cious very good to eat; tasting very good: **The strawberries are fresh and *delicious*.** [6]

de•sign **1.** a plan or sketch to be used as a pattern for making something: **This is the *design* I will use for my costume. 2.** a pattern of form or color: **The sweater's *design* is made of green and blue fish. 3.** to form a thing in a certain way: **to *design* a dress, to *design* a new computer.** [30]

did•n't a shorter way to say **did not**: **He was late and *didn't* get to the bus stop in time for his bus.** [26]

dis•ap•pear to go away or become hidden: **He does a magic trick in which he holds up a coin and then makes it *disappear*.** [28]

dis•cov•er to find out about something: **Scientists are still trying to *discover* a way to prevent the common cold.** [12]

dish•es plates or other objects used to serve food: **She helps out at home by washing the *dishes* after dinner.** [34]

dis•tance **1.** a point or place far away: **We could see the tallest buildings in the *distance*. 2.** how far it is between one place and another: **The *distance* from my house to school is about one mile.** [31]

does•n't a shorter way to say **does not**: **She stays out of the water because she *doesn't* know how to swim.** [26]

do•ing carrying on some action: **Laura is *doing* her homework in her room.** [28]

doll a toy that looks like a person: **Missy likes to pretend that her *doll* is a real baby.** [4]

dol•lar a unit of money that is the same as one hundred pennies: **Four quarters make one *dollar*.** [3]

don't a shorter way to say **do not**: **I *don't* watch TV on school nights.** [26]

door a part that moves so that you can go into or out of something: **You need a key to open the front *door* of our house.** [25]

down from a higher place to a lower one: **The ball rolled *down* the hill.** [30]

dress   1. a one-piece top and skirt that is worn by women and girls: **Janie got a new** *dress* **for her birthday. 2.** to put clothes on: **My little sister has learned to** *dress* **herself.** [15]

drew   made a picture with a pen, pencil, or crayon: **In art class today, Gene** *drew* **a picture of his pet rabbit.** [21]

dropped   to let fall; let go down: **I** *dropped* **a glass, and it broke on the floor.** [32]

dry   1. having very little water; not wet: **The Sahara Desert is a very** *dry* **place. 2.** to make dry: **She used a big towel to** *dry* **her hair after she had washed it.** [14]

duck

duck   a water bird with webbed feet and a broad bill: **A** *duck* **has feathers that keep off water.** [6]

dug   broke up the ground; made a hole in the ground: **We** *dug* **holes in the garden to plant our new rose bushes.** [6, 32]

each   one of two or more people or things: *Each* **question that you get right adds ten points to your score.** [9]

earn   1. to get money by doing work: **She can** *earn* **$6.00 per hour working at that store. 2.** to get what is deserved: **You will have to work hard to** *earn* **an A in that subject.** [3]

eat   to take in food; chew and swallow food: **They usually** *eat* **lunch at noon.** [9]

egg   a cell or cells produced by some female animals from which a young animal develops: **Birds, fish, and reptiles hatch from** *eggs*. [2]

ex•cit•ed   full of feeling: **The girls on the team were very** *excited* **when they scored the goal that won the game.** [20]

ex•plore   to go into new or unknown places: **The U.S. has sent spacecraft to** *explore* **the planet Mars.** [34]

F

fair   1. giving everyone the same chance: **Our teacher is** *fair* **and treats each student the same way. 2.** clear and sunny: **a** *fair* **spring day. 3.** a show where things are on display: **We all showed our science projects at the school science** *fair*. [9]

fall   1. the season of the year between summer and winter: *Fall* **is also called autumn. 2.** to go down suddenly from a higher place or position: **Be careful on those steps, or you will** *fall*. [15]

fa•mil•iar   well-known; often seen or heard: **All the people in this snapshot are** *familiar* **to me.** [7]

fam•i•ly   a group of people forming a household: **A new** *family* **just moved into the house across the street from us.** [7]

far   not near; at a great distance: **The road sign was too** *far* **away for her to read.** [24]

farm   land where plants or animals are raised for food: **My uncle has a** *farm* **in Iowa where he grows corn.** [24]

fast   moving quickly; going at a high speed: **Erin is a** *fast* **runner, and she wins all the races at school.** [14]

fav•o•rite   a person or thing that is liked the best: **When Li gets the newspaper, the first thing he reads is his** *favorite* **comic strip.** [16]

E
F

feel 1. to find out about by touching: **I can** *feel* **cold air coming in; there must be a window open somewhere.** 2. to have a certain sense in the body or mind: **to** *feel* **sick, to** *feel* **happy.** [9]

feet 1. the body parts at the end of the legs, used for standing and moving: **Humans and some animals stand on two** *feet.* 2. units of length, equal to 12 inches each: **Val's dad is over 6** *feet* **tall.** [9]

fes•ti•val a big party that takes place on a holiday or at another special time: **In the summer, our town has a** *festival* **of the arts with plays, concerts, and art shows.** [15]

field a piece of land used for sports: **Football is played on a** *field* **100 yards long.** [1]

fi•es•ta a day or time to celebrate something: **In Mexico a** *fiesta* **can be held to celebrate a religious holiday.** [15] ◆

◆ **Festival** and **fiesta** both mean the same thing. *Festival* is an English word, and *fiesta* is a Spanish word. Another word that means the same thing is **feast.** All these words go back to a Latin word meaning "a special holiday."

---

fight an attack with force or words: **Scott had a** *fight* **with his brother Ted after Ted called him a bad name.** [22]

fi•nal•ly at last: **I looked all over for my watch and** *finally* **found it next to the kitchen sink.** [34]

fin•ished completed: **When he** *finished* **writing his story, he checked it for spelling mistakes.** [25]

fire the flames, heat, and light given off by burning: **Someone dropped a match in the dry grass, and it started a** *fire.* [12]

fish 1. any of a large group of animals that live in the water: *Fish* **have fins to help them swim.** 2. to catch fish for food or as a sport: **We walked along the river looking for a good place to** *fish.* [16]

five the number that is one more than four; 5. [12]

fix to bring back to the proper condition; repair: **We had to** *fix* **Kevin's bicycle because the chain was broken.** [3]

fla•vor the seasoning of food; taste: **Chocolate ice cream has a wonderful** *flavor.* [27]

flew moved through the air by the use of wings: **The birds** *flew* **over the lake.** [21]

floor the bottom surface of a room: **There was a small rug on the** *floor.* [25]

fly 1. to move through the air by the use of wings: **Hawks** *fly* **high above the earth.** 2. a small insect with one pair of wings: **The** *fly* **is a common pest.** [14]

food what people and animals eat to keep them alive: **Pizza is a** *food* **that people often eat for lunch.** [21]

for 1. directed to a certain person or thing: **This picture book is** *for* **children.** 2. to a certain distance, time, or amount: **I slept** *for* **nine hours last night.** [27]

four the number that is one more than three; 4. [27]

fox a wild animal with a bushy tail and thick fur: **The** *fox* **is closely related to the wolf and the dog.** [4]

fox

from used to show a starting point or time: **I'll race you** *from* **here to our house. The store is open** *from* **nine o'clock in the morning until six o'clock at night.** [14]

fur•i•ous   very angry: **He was** *furious* **when he found out someone had picked all the flowers in the garden.** [22]

game   something that is done to have fun: **a** *game* **of cards, a** *game* **of checkers, a** *game* **of soccer.** [12]

gath•er   to come together at one place: **Even before the tickets went on sale, people began to** *gather* **around the ticket booth.** [14]

gen•tle   soft or mild: **She didn't get angry or upset but just spoke in a quiet,** *gentle* **voice.** [4]

get•ting   **1.** going onto or into: **Manuel tripped as he was** *getting* **on the bus. 2.** coming to have: **I'm** *getting* **a new bike because my old one is too small. 3.** becoming: **It was** *getting* **dark, and they had to stop the game.** [32]

gi•gan•tic   very big; huge: **Many dinosaurs were** *gigantic* **animals.** [8]

girls   female children; children who are not boys: **There are fifteen** *girls* **in the fourth-grade class.** [34]

giv•ing   letting have as a present: **What are you** *giving* **Maria for her birthday?** [33]

glass   **1.** a hard material that can be seen through and breaks easily: *Glass* **is made by melting together sand and certain other materials. 2.** a container made of this material, used for drinking: **I'd like a** *glass* **of milk, please.** [15]

glide   to move in a smooth, easy way: **Some kinds of planes can** *glide* **through the air without using power.** [10]

glow   to shine with a soft, clear light: **The eyes of a cat seem to** *glow* **in the dark when light hits them.** [28]

go•ing   moving from one place to an-

other: **What time are you** *going* **to see the movie?** [28]

grabbed   took something in a sudden way: **Before anyone else could take the last piece of candy, Jerry** *grabbed* **it and put it in his mouth.** [32]

grand•ma   the mother of a person's mother or father: *Grandma* **is a name that children call their grandmother.** [31]

grass   any of a large family of green plants with long, thin leaves: *Grass* **is a plant that grows all over the world.** [14]

grew   became bigger: **Andrew** *grew* **five inches taller in the past year.** [21]

group   a number of persons or things together: **Tigers usually live alone, but lions live together in a** *group.* [21]

had   the form of the word **have** we use to tell about the past: **Willy** *had* **to leave school early yesterday.** [1]

hard   **1.** not easy to do or understand: **The science test was** *hard,* **and no one got an 'A' on it. 2.** solid and firm; not easy to push in or bend: **Diana hurt her knee when she fell on the** *hard* **sidewalk.** [24]

harm•less   not causing harm or damage: **That looks like a real sword, but it is actually just a** *harmless* **toy made of rubber.** [34]

heart   the large muscle that pumps blood to all parts of the body: **Your** *heart* **is in your chest.** [24] ♦

♦ **Heart** is the muscle that pumps blood to the body. The word also has many other meanings coming from the idea that the heart is the most important part of the body. For example, the *heart* of a city is the most important part of the city.

her•self   her own self: **She's old enough now to cross the street by *herself*.** [31]

he's   a shorter way to say **he is: If Eric doesn't hurry, *he's* going to be late for school.** [20]

hid   put out of sight: **Mark *hid* the present for Susan in the back of his closet.** [3]

high   going far above the ground; not low: **That mountain looks very *high* from here.** [22]

hill   a piece of ground that is higher than the land around it but smaller than a mountain: **When it snows, we ride sleds down the *hill* behind our house.** [3]

him   a male person who is being talked about: **I called Chuck on the phone and asked *him* about our math homework.** [3]

him•self   his own self: **Josh is lucky he didn't hurt *himself* when he fell down the stairs.** [31]

hope   to want something to happen or be true: **I *hope* the weather will be nice for our picnic tomorrow.** [13]

horse   a large animal that has four legs: **A *horse* is strong and can run very fast.** [25]

how   in what way: **Can you tell me *how* to get to Main Street from here?** [30]

huge   very large: **The whale is a *huge* animal.** [13]

if   in the event that: ***If* it rains today, the game will be put off until Tuesday.** [3]

I'll   a shorter way to say **I will: I have to go now, or *I'll* be late for dinner.** [20]

I'm   a shorter way to say **I am: *I'm* sorry that I stepped on your foot.** [20]

im•por•tant   worth extra attention:

Eating good foods is *important* if you want to stay healthy. [15]

inch•es   small units of length: **There are twelve *inches* in one foot.** [34]

I've   a shorter way to say **I have: I like that movie, and *I've* seen it twice.** [26]

job   work for which a person is paid: **The *job* of a firefighter is to put out fires.** [4]

join   **1.** to become a member of a group: **Bobby wants to *join* the Boy Scouts. 2.** to get together with someone: **She told all the children to *join* hands in a circle.** [14]

jump   to use the legs to move up in the air: **Basketball players *jump* high to catch or shoot the ball.** [6]

keep   **1.** to continue or maintain: ***Keep* your hands on the handlebars to be safe. 2.** to have and hold onto: **She's just going to borrow the book, not *keep* it.** [9]

ket•tle   a large pot used to heat liquids or cook food: **a *kettle* of soup.** [27]

kick   to hit with the foot: **Soccer players try to *kick* the ball into the goal.** [19]

kind   **1.** wanting to help others; friendly: **Helping Mrs. Smith with her packages was a *kind* thing to do. 2.** a group of things that are the same in some way; a type: **Owls are one *kind* of bird.** [7]

laid   **1.** produced an egg: **We gathered the eggs the duck had *laid*. 2.** put down on a surface: **When he was finished digging, he *laid* his shovel on the ground.** [8]

larg•er bigger: **Your feet are** *larger* **than mine.** [21]

last 1. coming after all others: **December is the** *last* **month of the year. 2.** to stay in good condition: **That battery should** *last* **for at least one year.** [14]

late not on time: **He missed the bus and was** *late* **for school.** [12]

lay to place or put down on a surface: **You can** *lay* **the box down on the table.** [8]

leg 1. one of the body parts used to walk or run: **The knee is part of the** *leg.* **2.** a part that supports something: **the** *leg* **of a table.** [2]

less not as much: **His dad wants him to spend** *less* **time watching TV and more time studying.** [15]

let's a shorter way to say **let us:** *Let's* **take the bus home.** [26]

life the quality that makes people, animals, and plants able to grow and produce new living things like themselves: **Rocks and machines do not have** *life.* [12]

light 1. the opposite of darkness: **The sun gives off a very bright** *light.* **2.** to make burn: **I used a match to** *light* **the candles. 3.** not heavy: **A paper towel is very** *light.* [22, 28]

lightning

light•ning a sudden flash of light in the sky that happens during a storm: *Lightning* **is actually a form of electricity.** [31]

liked felt good about; enjoyed: **I** *liked* **the book and want to read another one by the same author.** [33]

lis•ten to pay attention to a sound: **Mom likes to** *listen* **to the news on the radio.** [4]

live•ly active; full of life: **Our new puppy is very** *lively* **and loves to run and play.** [19]

liv•ing having life: **Although many dinosaurs were bigger, the elephant is the largest** *living* **land animal.** [33]

long 1. having great length; not short: **Our dog has a** *long* **tail. 2.** being a great distance from one end to the other: **It is a** *long* **way across the Atlantic Ocean.** [18]

looked used the eyes to see: **He** *looked* **out the window and saw his friend coming up the street.** [28]

look•ing using the eyes for seeing: **If you are** *looking* **for your book, I saw it on the kitchen table.** [28]

loom a machine or frame used to make cloth: **Cotton cloth is made by a huge machine called a power** *loom.* [30]

lot 1. a large amount: **A** *lot* **of people watch the Super Bowl football game on TV. 2.** a piece of land: **They are going to build a house on that empty** *lot.* [4]

loved had a strong feeling of caring for someone or something; liked very much: **The story of Little Red Riding Hood tells how she** *loved* **her grandmother.** [33]

low 1. near to the ground or another surface: **The plane was flying very** *low,* **just over the houses below. 2.** not high in amount: **Ninety cents is a** *low* **price for a gallon of gas.** [10]

mad feeling anger; angry: **Joey is** *mad* **at Susan because she didn't invite him to her party.** [1]

made formed into something: **Jamala** *made* **a whistle out of clay.** [12]

M

make to form into something: **She is going to** *make* **a pie for dessert.** [12]

mam•mal the name used in science for an animal that has a backbone, is warm-blooded, and has hair or fur on the body: **A female** *mammal* **gives birth to live young and feeds them with her milk.** [21]

mammal

map a drawing or chart that shows a certain place and its important features: **When we drove to Florida, we used a road** *map* **to tell us where to go.** [1]

ma•ter•i•al cloth: **Cotton is a** *material* **that is often used for clothing.** [24]

math a shorter word for **mathematics,** the study of numbers: **In** *math* **class, students learn to add and subtract.** [18]

may a helping verb that means: **1.** it is more or less likely: **We** *may* **get there by lunchtime; it depends on how much traffic there is. 2.** it is allowed: **Students** *may* **play outside after they eat lunch.** [8]

me the person who is speaking or writing: **I asked Jed to call** *me* **at home later.** [7]

med•i•cine something that is taken into or put on the body to bring back good health: **When people are sick, they often take** *medicine* **to get better.** [12]

mem•ber a person or animal that belongs to a certain group: **Heather is a** *member* **of the Girl Scouts.** [21]

men more than one man: *Men* **who work in a business office usually wear a necktie to work.** [2]

mess a place that is dirty and has things scattered about: **His room was a big** *mess,* **with dirty clothes and toys all over the floor.** [2]

might **1.** a helping verb that means something more or less likely: **Peggy** *might* **come for dinner, so Mom bought some extra meat. 2.** strength or power: **Lily kicked the ball with all her** *might.* [22]

milk a white liquid that comes from mother animals to feed their young: **People use** *milk* **to make cheese and butter.** [19]

miss to not do, see, or know: **In baseball it is a strike if you swing and** *miss* **the ball.** [15]

mom a friendly name for a mother: **My** *mom* **leaves my breakfast for me before she goes to work.** [4]

more greater than another in number or amount: **In baseball the team that scores** *more* **runs wins the game.** [25]

most **1.** greatest in number or amount: **California has the** *most* **people of any state in the U.S. 2.** to a great amount; nearly all: *Most* **of the children I know like to play tag.** [7]

move to go to a new place: **Please** *move* **your car because it is blocking our driveway.** [13]

mov•ing going from one place to another: **The people in line were** *moving* **very slowly.** [33]

much being a large amount: **I'd rather watch a movie in the theater than on TV because the screen is** *much* **bigger.** [6]

mud dirt that is wet and sticky: **Get the** *mud* **off your shoes before you come into the house.** [6]

mule

mule an animal that is part horse and part donkey: **A** *mule* **has longer ears than a horse.** [13]

must   a helping verb that means something is certain or likely: **These footprints** *must* **belong to our dog.** [6]

my   belonging to me: *My* **brother and I sleep in the same bedroom.** [7]

neck   the body part that connects the head to the body: **A swan has a long, graceful** *neck.* [19]

need   to want or require something: **Plants** *need* **water and light to grow.** [9]

new   made or done now or a short time ago; not old: **She bought a** *new* **dress at the store. When spring comes, trees grow** *new* **leaves.** [21]

nice   good or pleasing in some way: **Our soccer coach is a** *nice* **woman who never yells at us.** [12]

night   the time when it is dark; the time between sunset and sunrise: **Some animals sleep during the day and come out to hunt at** *night.* [22]

noise   a sound: **The saw made a loud** *noise* **as it cut through the wood.** [34]

nose   the part of the face or head that is used for breathing and smelling: **A dog depends on its** *nose* **to find things.** [13]

note   a short letter or message: **Mom left us a** *note* **to say that she went to the store to buy milk.** [13]

once   one time: **My favorite TV show is on** *once* **a week, on Friday afternoon.** [2]

or   a special word used to show a choice: **1.** one of a group of things: **Would you like a red, a blue,** *or* **a green ribbon on your package? 2.** the second of two things: **Send the card today,** *or* **it won't get there in time.** [25]

oth•er   not this one: **Our team had six points in the game, and the** *other* **team had five.** [30]

out   away from the inside: **It was a nice day, and Lisa went** *out* **to play.** [30]

o•ver   **1.** higher than; above: **The ball went** *over* **the fence. 2.** at the end: **We left the theater when the movie was** *over.* [30]

own   **1.** belonging to oneself or itself: **The puppy sleeps in its** *own* **little bed. 2.** to have something belong to one: **Mr. and Mrs. Davis** *own* **a store where they sell toys and games.** [10]

pack   **1.** a large bundle, to be carried on a person or animal: **Gina's** *pack* **was full of books. 2.** to put something into a box or suitcase: **Be sure to** *pack* **some warm clothes for your trip. 3.** a group of things that belong together: **a** *pack* **of cards, a** *pack* **of wolves.** [19]

pack•age   something packed, wrapped up, or tied together: **Teri got a** *package* **in the mail from our uncle.** [8]

paint•ing   completed picture done with paint: **I used watercolor paints when I made this** *painting.* [25]

pal•ace   a huge building in which a king or other ruler lives. **Queen Elizabeth of Great Britain lives in a** *palace* **in London.** ♦ [26]

♦ **Palace** is a word that comes from a place in the ancient city of Rome. The Palatine Hill Hill was a hill at the center of the city of Rome. The ruler of Rome lived there in a large building. *Palace* meant "the house of the ruler on Palatine Hill."

park   1. an area of land set aside for everyone to use: **I like to go to the *park* after school to play ball or ride my bike.** 2. to leave a car for a time in a special place: **Dad didn't stop at the store because he couldn't find a place to *park*.** [24]

part   something that belongs to a thing but is not all of it: **The first *part* of the movie was good, but it got boring later on.** [24]

pass   to go beyond: **He drove faster to *pass* the car in front of him.** [15]

pay   to give money to buy something or for work done: **Mom is going to *pay* me five dollars to shovel all the snow off the driveway.** [8]

peo•ple   more than one person; a group of persons: **About 10,000 *people* live in this town.** [13]

per•fect   with nothing wrong; as good as it can be: **Tyrone drew a *perfect* picture of his kitten.** ♦ [6]

♦ **Perfect** means that something is as good as it can possibly be. Sometimes people use the word just to mean "very good," as in: **That was really a *perfect* meal we had for dinner last night.** But to be really correct, you should use *perfect* to mean "the best that it can ever be."

---

phone   a shorter word for **telephone: I want to call Mom on the *phone* to ask if I can eat dinner at Stacy's house.** [3]

pin   a short length of metal with a point at one end and a flat head at the other: **She put her name tag on with a *pin*.** [3]

placed   put something in a certain position: **He *placed* the bowl of flowers in the center of the table.** [33]

plan   ideas about what to do or how to do something: **The coach has a *plan* for how we can win the game.** [13]

planned   worked out how to do something: **The trip went just as they had**

planned, **and they arrived right on time.** [32]

play   1. to make music on an instrument: **to *play* the piano, to *play* the guitar.** 2. to have fun: **We love to *play* outside at recess.** [14]

play•ing   doing something for fun: **The children were in the yard, *playing* a game of tag.** [28]

pond   a small, shallow body of water: **Fish, frogs, and ducks live in the little *pond* near our house.** [4]

pond

pop•ping   making a short, sudden sound: **The engine made a funny *popping* sound, but it wouldn't start.** [32]

prac•tice   to do something over and over to get better at it: **to *practice* the piano, to *practice* throwing a baseball.** [1]

prob•lem   something that is hard to figure out or that causes trouble: **We had a *problem* when we brought the new sofa home, because it was too big to fit through the front door.** [8]

put•ting   placing in a certain spot: **Katie spends hours *putting* toy blocks into her wagon and then dumping them out.** [32]

rain   1. drops of water that fall from clouds: **We had more than an inch of *rain* from last night's storm.** 2. to fall as water in this way: **Those dark clouds make me think it's going to *rain* today.** [8]

reach   1. to stretch out the arm to try to touch or hold something: **Can you *reach* the top shelf to get down that bowl? 2.** to go as far as a certain place: **Our plane should *reach* Chicago at about two o'clock.** [16]

read   to look at something that is written and understand it: **Children usually learn to *read* when they are about six years old.** [9] ♦

~~~

♦ **Read** is an unusual word because the same word is used to talk about the present (now) and about the past (then): **I like to *read* books about animals.** (now) **Last week I *read* a book about lions.** (then) The two words are spelled the same but have different sounds. Now I <u>read</u> a book has a sound like "need." Then I <u>read</u> a book has a sound like "red."

~~~

rich   having a lot of money: **Movie stars can get *rich* from the films they make.** [16]

rid•ing   sitting on or in something and making it move: **Carrie was *riding* her bike in the park when she got a flat tire.** [33]

right   1. on the side opposite the left: **Most people write with their *right* hand. 2.** without a mistake; correct: **Sandy had all the *right* answers on the test.** [22]

ring   1. a band in the shape of a circle that is worn on a finger: **Maggie has a gold *ring* that she wears on her right hand. 2.** to make a sound like a bell: **We have to go in from recess when we hear the bell *ring*.** [18]

road   a smooth strip of ground that has been cleared so that cars or other vehicles can go on it: **Route 5 is the main *road* across the state of Kansas.** [10]

rock   1. to move back and forth or side to side: **If you *rock* the cradle, the baby will fall asleep. 2.** the solid material that makes up part of the earth's crust: **The house is built on solid *rock*. 3.** a small piece of this material: **He threw a *rock* into the water, and it made a big splash.** [4]

room   1. an area in a building that is set aside for a particular use: **Our school has a computer *room* where we can do word processing. 2.** the space that is needed for something: **There is enough *room* in the garage to park two cars.** [21]

rope   a thick, strong cord made of twisted or woven strands of wire or fiber: **A *rope* can be used to pull heavy things.** [13]

round   shaped like a circle or ball: **An orange is a *round* fruit.** [16]

row   1. to use oars to move a boat: **It took us about twenty minutes to *row* across the lake. 2.** a straight line of people or things: **We sat in the last *row* of the theater to watch the movie.** [10]

run•ning   faster than when walking; going by moving the legs quickly: **In baseball after you hit the ball, you start *running* to first base.** ♦ [32]

~~~

♦ **Run** is probably the word in English with the most different meanings. If you look in a large dictionary, you will find that **run** has as many as one hundred meanings. Some of these are a *run* in baseball, a *run* of bad luck, a *run* on a bank, to *run* a business, to *run* a computer, and to *run* a story in a newspaper.

~~~

S

sad   not happy; feeling bad: **Rashon was *sad* when his new toy broke the first time he played with it.** [1]

sat got into a still position in a chair: **When Mom said dinner was ready, I went and** *sat* **at the table.** [1]

saved kept for a later time: **They didn't eat all the meat, so they** *saved* **the rest to use for sandwiches.** [33]

say to speak words out loud: **People usually** *say* **"Hello" when they answer the telephone.** [8]

school a place for learning and teaching: **Children go to** *school* **to learn to read and write.** [21]

scis•sors a tool with two blades used for cutting: **He used a pair of** *scissors* **to cut the piece of string.** [24]

seat a place to sit: **The teacher changed my** *seat,* **and now I sit next to Juan.** [9]

seesaw

see•saw a long board that is balanced on a bar: **Children play on a** *seesaw* **in a playground.** [31]

set 1. to put something in a certain place: *Set* **those packages down on the kitchen table. 2.** a group of things that belong together: **a** *set* **of dishes.** [2]

sew to make clothes or other things with a needle and thread: **She had to** *sew* **a button on her jacket.** [27]

sew•ing the act of someone who sews: **This machine is used for** *sewing* **clothes.** [24]

shape the outer form of something: **These cookies have a round** *shape.* [16]

she's a shorter way to say **she is: Jessie called and said that** *she's* **on her way home.** [20]

ship

ship 1. a large boat that goes on the ocean: **The** <u>Titanic</u> **is a famous** *ship* **that sank the first time it ever went to sea. 2.** to send a thing from one place to another: **Farmers grow oranges in Florida and** *ship* **them to other parts of the country.** [16]

shoot 1. to try to score a goal in games such as basketball, soccer, or hockey: **When players are fouled in basketball, they sometimes** *shoot* **a basket. 2.** to fire a gun or other weapon: **She knows how to** *shoot* **arrows with a bow.** [9]

shop 1. a small store: **We get our cat's food at the pet** *shop* **in our neighborhood. 2.** to go to stores to look at and buy things: **Theresa loves to** *shop* **for clothes.** [16]

short not tall or long: **Two seconds is a** *short* **time.** [25]

show 1. to bring into sight: **Mr. Gray is going to** *show* **a movie in class tomorrow. 2.** something that is seen by people: **We're going to the auto** *show* **to see what next year's cars will look like.** [10]

side a part of something that is not the top, bottom, front, or back: **The driver of a car gets in and out of a car on the left** *side.* [12]

sight 1. something to see: **The clowns in the circus were a funny *sight* in their odd costumes. 2.** the power to see: **Dad got glasses for reading because his *sight* isn't as good as it used to be.** [22]

sit to be in a position in which the body rests on the hips: **Please *sit* still in your chair. Danny was *sitting* on the bench waiting for a chance to get into the game.** [3, 32]

six the number that is one more than five; 6. [3]

sky the space above the earth: **The clouds floated across the *sky*.** [22]

sled a plastic disk or wooden vehicle with runners that carries people over the snow: **Pablo rode his *sled* down the snowy hill.** [14]

slipped moved suddenly or slid out of control: **Amy *slipped* on the ice and sat down hard.** [32]

slow going at a low speed; not fast: **Five miles an hour is a fast speed for walking, but it is a *slow* speed for a car. ♦** [10]

♦ **Slow** can be used in several different ways without any change in the word. It can tell about a person or a thing: **He is a *slow* eater and is always the last one to finish his lunch.** It can show action: **Cars had to *slow* down because of the heavy traffic.** And it can tell how an action happens: **Go *slow* when you get to the corner.** This last use can also be written as **slowly: Go *slowly* when you get to the corner.**

---

snore to make a loud, rough noise while sleeping: **I thought Dad was just resting until I heard him start to *snore*.** [18]

so **1.** in the same way: **I liked the movie, and *so* did my friends. 2.** with the result that: **All the seats were taken, *so* we had to stand.** [27]

soar to fly quickly and easily: **A hawk can *soar* high above the earth.** [10]

some•thing a thing that is not known or named: ***Something* got stuck in the sink, and now the water won't run out.** [31]

some•times now and then: ***Sometimes* we eat breakfast in the dining room.** [31]

some•where in or to a place that is not known or named: **When we go to the beach, we like to put our blanket down *somewhere* near the water.** [31]

soon before long: **I'm really hungry, and I hope dinner will be ready *soon*.** [21]

sort **1.** a group of things that are somewhat alike: **What *sort* of books do you like to read? 2.** to arrange by kind: **After she washed the socks, she had to *sort* them into pairs.** [25]

sound something that is sensed by the ears: **Did you hear the *sound* of thunder?** [4]

sow to plant or scatter seeds in order to grow plants: **The farmer will *sow* wheat in his fields.** [27]

squawk•ing making a loud, sharp cry: **Alex says his parrot is talking, but it sounds to me like *squawking*.** [20]

start **1.** to go into action; begin: **The game will *start* at two o'clock and end at about four o'clock. 2.** the first part; the beginning: **Let's sit here so that we can see the *start* of the race.** [24]

start•ed to make a beginning; set out: **The hikers *started* on their trip in the rain.** [28]

stew a thick soup: **Beef *stew* is made with small pieces of beef and vegetables.** [6]

stick a long, thin piece of wood: **I threw the *stick*, and my dog ran after it.** [19]

still **1.** without movement or sound; quietly: **The rabbit heard a noise and stood *still*, listening for where it came from. 2.** as before; even now: **Do you *still* want to go, even though it might rain?** [14]

S

stood   stayed in one place on the feet: **Marta** *stood* **up to make her speech.** [14]

stop   to keep from moving or doing something: **Could you please** *stop* **talking?** [4]

stopped   kept from moving or doing something: **The car** *stopped* **when the light turned red.** [32]

store   a place where things are sold: **I got this shirt at a** *store* **in the mall.** [25]

storm   a heavy rain or snow with strong winds: **More than six inches of snow fell during last night's** *storm.* [31]

storm

stretch   1. to extend the body or a part of it: **Kim likes to** *stretch* **her legs before she runs. 2.** to make longer: **You can** *stretch* **a rubber band so that it becomes much longer.** [18]

sup•per   a meal eaten in the evening: **We had dinner in the afternoon and then a light** *supper* **at night.** [27]

sur•face   1. the top of the water, where the water meets the air: **There are bugs on the** *surface* **of the pond. 2.** the outside or top of something: **The car wash does not use brushes because brushes can scratch the** *surface* **of a car.** [33]

tail   a movable part of an animal's body that sticks out from the rear: **Our dog wags his** *tail* **whenever he is happy.** [8]

take   1. to travel by: **Do you** *take* **a bus to school? 2.** to get hold of: *Take* **my hand when we cross the street.** [12]

tak•ing   carrying: **My little brother is** *taking* **his favorite toy along on our trip.** [33]

tan•gled   twisted and trapped: **When she got out of bed, her hair was all** *tangled,* **and she had a hard time combing it.** [33] ◆

◆ Tangle once had a different meaning than the meaning it has now. It meant a kind of seaweed. This may appear to have no connection with the present meaning, but actually it isn't as far off as it seems. This seaweed grew in a wild, tangled way, and people began to use *tangle* to talk about other things that looked like this.

tape   1. to fasten or bind with tape: **Ask Andrew to** *tape* **this ripped book cover. 2.** a long, narrow strip of plastic, paper, or cloth that is sticky on one side: *Tape* **is used to wrap packages or close boxes.** [8]

taste   1. to get the flavor of something: **She has to** *taste* **the sauce to see whether it is ready. 2.** flavor; what makes food different and special in your mouth: **Strawberries have a sweet** *taste.* [27]

team   a group of people who play on the same side in a game: **The Boston Red Sox is a famous baseball** *team.* [1, 9]

ten   the number that is one more than nine; 10. [2]

than   a word used to compare one thing with another or others: **I like pizza better** *than* **any other food.** [18]

that's   a shorter way to say **that is:** *That's* **our car parked across the street from the school.** [20]

their   belonging to them: **The people who live next door to us have a big oak tree in** *their* **yard.** [27]

them　the people or things being talked or written about: **The Smiths asked us whether we wanted to go with** *them* **to the zoo.** [18]

there　**1.** at that place: **You sit here, and I'll sit over** *there* **by the window. 2.** it is true; it is a fact: *There* **are thirty days in the month of June.** [27]

there's　a shorter way to say **there is:** *There's* **a strange dog in our yard.** [20]

they　the people or things being talked or written about: **The children got wet when** *they* **were playing out in the rain.** [18]

they're　a shorter way to say **they are:** **There is a** For Sale **sign on their lawn, so I guess** *they're* **going to move.** [20]

things　**1.** objects or items: **Books, pencils, and paper are** *things* **you use in school. 2.** subjects or ideas: **From that movie, I learned a lot of interesting** *things* **about how whales live.** [34]

those　showing the people or things that are being talked or written about: **We want to save** *those* **papers in the box.** [18]

thread　a very thin string or cord that is used in sewing: **Elias used black** *thread* **to sew the rip in his black sweater.** [24]

throne　a large, decorated chair that a king or queen sits on: **The queen sat on a** *throne* **when she met with her court.** [26]

throw•ing　tossing: **The pitcher starts the play in baseball by** *throwing* **the ball to the batter.** [20]

times　**1.** certain points or periods in history; occasions: **He's already seen that movie three** *times* **before, but he still likes to watch it. 2.** multiplied by: **Two** *times* **three is six.** [34]

to　in the direction of: **The bus takes them** *to* **school. Please take this note** *to* **the teacher.** [27]

told　made known to someone: **My uncle** *told* **me a funny joke about a dog that**

could talk. [7]

too　in addition to; also: **I'd like an apple, and Craig wants one,** *too***.** [27]

took　**1.** got hold of; came to have: **When I passed around the cookies, Debbie** *took* **two. 2.** carried or went along with: **He** *took* **the garbage out and put it in the garbage can.** [19]

top　the highest part of something: **There was snow on the** *top* **of the mountain.** [4]

toss　to throw: **I'll** *toss* **this ball in the air, and you try to catch it.** [9]

touch　**1.** to feel something by using a part of the body: **Don't** *touch* **that wall with your hand because the paint is still wet. 2.** to put one thing up against something else: **The desk should be very close to the wall but should not** *touch* **it.** [4]

to•ward　in the direction of; near: **At night many kinds of insects will go** *toward* **a bright light and fly around it.** [9]

toys　things that children play with for fun: **Charlie has a big box in his room to put all his** *toys* **in.** [34]

track　**1.** a mark or footprint left on the ground by an animal or person as it moves: **If you look closely, you can see a** *track* **in the snow that was left by a deer. 2.** the rails that a train runs on: **The trains that run on this** *track* **go to the city.** [19]

train　**1.** a line of railroad cars joined together and pulled by an engine: **At this station, you can get a** *train* **that will take you all the way to California. 2.** to teach how to do something: **Michael wants to** *train* **his dog to bring in the newspaper.** [8]

trou•ble　**1.** problem; difficulty: **Jeff got in** *trouble* **at school because he was teasing a younger boy. 2.** extra work or effort: **I hope Mom likes this present, because I went to a lot of** *trouble* **to find it.** [22]

try　**1.** to make an effort to do something;

attempt: **We *try* to learn a new word every day. 2.** an effort to do something; an attempt: **Jill didn't get the ball in the goal, but it was a good *try* anyway.** [7]

try•ing   making an effort to do something: **My baby sister is *trying* to learn to walk.** [28]

tune   simple songs that are easy to remember: **Our teacher made up a class song to the *tune* of "Mary Had a Little Lamb."** [14]

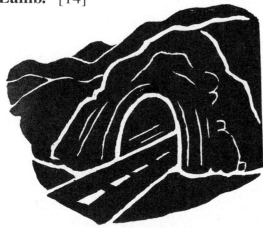

tunnel

tun•nel   a long, narrow passage under the ground or the water: **Cars can drive under the river by going through a *tunnel*.** [32]

turn   1. a chance for one person to do something: **Each child was given one *turn* in the game. 2.** to move in a circle or part of a circle: **You *turn* this knob to the right to make the radio louder. 3.** to change in some way: **As the sun went down, the air began to *turn* cold. 4.** a movement in a circle or part of a circle: **Make a left *turn* at the next corner.**

two   the number that is more than one and less than three; 2. [27]

un•cle   the brother of someone's mother or father: **The husband of your aunt is**

also called your *uncle*. [7]

up•on   touching and held up by; on: **She placed the vase of flowers *upon* the table.** [31]

us   the persons who are speaking or writing: **Dad drove *us* to the movies.** [6]

use   1. to put into action or service for some purpose: **We will *use* the good dishes for dinner tonight, since we are having company. 2.** the act or fact of being in service: **All the pay phones were in *use*, and he had to wait to make his call.** [13]

used   1. put into action for some purpose: **She *used* a knife to cut open the package. 2.** not new: **A *used* car is one that has already been owned by some other person.** [33]

ver•y   more than usual: **In most of the U.S., it gets cold in the winter; in Alaska it gets *very* cold.** [30]

wait   1. to stay in a place until someone comes or something happens: **We will *wait* right here until the next bus comes. 2.** the time spent doing this: **They had a long *wait* before the bus finally came.** [8]

want•ed   wished to have or do something: **Barbara has *wanted* to be an airplane pilot ever since she was a child.** [28]

wash   1. to get rid of dirt or stains with water, or with soap and water: **It's your turn to *wash* the dishes tonight. 2.** the clothes or other things that are cleaned at one time: **She put a large load of *wash* into the washing machine.** [16]

was•n't   a shorter way to say **was not: I**

called my friend Li on the phone, but she *wasn't* at home. [26]

way   1. a certain method to do or get something: **My coach showed me the right *way* to pitch a ball so that I wouldn't hurt my arm. 2.** a road or path that leads from one place to another: **Route 7 is the fastest *way* to drive to the city from here.** [8]

weath•er   the way things are outside; sunny, rainy, cold, hot, and so on: **Southern California usually has warm, dry *weather* during the summer.** ♦ [31]

♦ **Weather** comes from a word that means "storm." We now use the word for nice, sunny days as well as for rainy or snowy days. But in early times, it was during storms that people really noticed what the weather was like. So they used **weather** as another word for **storm.**

---

weave   to make cloth by lacing threads over and under each other: **A Native American visitor taught us how to *weave* baskets out of thin strips of wood.** [30]

were   a form of the word **be** that we use to talk about more than one person or thing in the past: **We are now learning about fish in our science class; last week we *were* studying insects.** [30]

we're   a shorter way to say **we are:** **Mom promised me that *we're* going to take a vacation trip this summer.** [20]

wet   covered or soaked with water or another liquid: **The streets were *wet* after the sudden heavy rain.** [2]

whale

whale   a very large animal that lives in water: **A *whale* is actually a mammal, not a fish.** [33]

what's   a shorter way to say **what is** or **what has:** *What's* the name of that boy who's in your car pool? [20]

which   what one or ones: *Which* of the books do you want to read first? [18]

while   1. a short period of time: **They got tired of walking and sat down to rest for a *while*. 2.** during the time that: **We don't like to get phone calls *while* we're eating dinner.** [18]

win   1. to be first or best in a game or contest: **Karen has to spell one more word correctly to *win* the spelling bee. 2.** to get as a prize in a game or contest: **The person who guesses the number will *win* two free tickets to the play.** [3]

wish   1. to hope very much for something: **I *wish* the rain would stop because I want to go out to play. 2.** something that a person hopes for: **If you could have just one *wish*, what would you choose? In the fairy tale, the prince was given three *wishes*.** [16, 34]

woke   went from sleeping to not sleeping: **She *woke* early in the morning and dressed quickly.** [13]

won't   a shorter way to say **will not: If you can be there by five o'clock, you *won't* be late.** [26]

wool   the thick, soft hair taken from sheep or some kinds of goats and used to make clothing: ***Wool* is used to make warm sweaters and coats.** [30]

wool

work **1.** the act or fact of working: **It took a lot of** *work* **to build this house. 2.** to do a job: **He had to** *work* **hard on his science project. 3.** to act or operate in the proper way: **This flashlight will not** *work* **unless you put in a new battery.** [3]

would•n't a shorter way to say **would not: I had to do all the work alone because he** *wouldn't* **help me.** [26]

yes a word that shows agreement; the opposite of "no:" *Yes,* **I do want to go.** [2]

yet up to this time; so far: **I want to read that book, but I haven't had time** *yet.* [2]

you the person or persons who are being spoken or written to: *You* **don't have to buy the book; I will lend** *you* **mine. 2.** a person; anyone: *You* **have to be 7 years old to go to this camp.** [21]

you're a shorter way to say **you are: If** *you're* **finished with the newspaper, I'd like to read it now.** [20]

THE WRITING PROCESS

In writing, you can use a plan called the *writing process* to help you think of ideas and then write about them. These are the parts of the writing process.

PREWRITING
Think about what you want to write about. Think about who will read your story. Then choose a topic. Plan your writing with a list, a drawing, or a web.

DRAFTING
Put your ideas in writing. Don't worry about making mistakes. You can fix them later.

RESPONDING AND REVISING
Meet with a partner or group to talk about your writing. Then make any changes that will make your writing better.

PROOFREADING
Correct any mistakes you find.

PUBLISHING
Share your writing. Decide how you want to publish your work.

TIPS FOR USING THE WRITING PROCESS

When you write, remember . . .

Prewriting

What will you write about? You might write about something that happened to you, something you already know about, or something you would like to know more about.

Choose a topic. Then plan your writing. Try listing ideas, or make a story map, a web, or a drawing.

Drafting

Begin writing your first draft. Use the plan you made to help you write. Just get your ideas down on paper. You can make changes later.

Look at the next page for more about the writing process.

Responding and Revising

Now ask your writing partner or group to read what you have written. Ask for ideas to help you make your writing better.

Make only the changes you think will make your writing better.

I like Jason's idea. I think I'll change the ending of my story.

PROOFREADING CHECKLIST

☑ Circle any words you are not sure you spelled correctly. Look them up in a dictionary, or ask someone who knows how to spell them.

☑ Look for words you have misspelled before. Add them to your Spelling Log.

☑ If you are unsure of how to spell a word, try saying the word slowly. Listen to every syllable. Did you write all the syllables?

☑ Check your capitalization and punctuation.

I'm not sure how to spell this word. I'll circle it and look it up in the dictionary.

Proofreading

Now make the changes you have decided to make. Proofread your writing. Use editor's marks to mark the mistakes you find. Also mark any other changes you want to make. Use the Proofreading Checklist to help you.

SPELLING STRATEGIES

Welcome to our classroom! Let us show you some of our favorite spelling strategies!

When I'm learning to spell a word, I use the Study Steps to Learn a Word. They're on pages 8 and 9 of your book.

Try this tip to help you spell a word! Say the word. Then close your eyes and picture the way it is spelled. Think about whether some of the letter pairs spell a single sound.

I like to proofread my work twice. The first time, I circle words I know are misspelled. Then I go back and look for words I'm not sure of.

I think of ways to spell the vowel sound in a word. Then I try different spellings.

grean? green?

Sometimes I read the words backward. I start with the last word and end with the first word.

To help me remember how to spell <u>ready</u>, I remember it has the word <u>read</u> in it.

When I need to spell <u>eight</u>, I think of this silly sentence: <u>E</u>ven <u>I</u>rving's <u>g</u>eese <u>h</u>onk <u>t</u>oday. Put together the first letter of each, and you have <u>eight</u>!

Drawing the shape of a word helps me remember how to spell it. This is the shape of the word <u>park</u>.

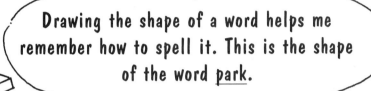

When I don't know how to spell a word, sometimes I think of a word that rhymes with it. Both words may have the same spelling pattern.

We are proofreading partners! She reads the words aloud while I look at the spelling. Then we trade jobs.

If you don't know how to spell a word, you might just take a guess! Then you can check the dictionary to see if you were right!

Sometimes I look up a word in the dictionary. Sometimes I just ask someone how to spell it.

MY

SPELLING LOG

What's a Spelling Log?

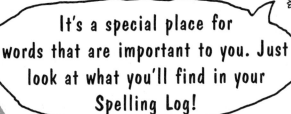

It's a special place for words that are important to you. Just look at what you'll find in your Spelling Log!

WORDS TO STUDY

pages 180–183

This is just the place for you to list words you need to study. There is a box for each unit of your spelling book.

MY OWN WORD COLLECTION

pages 188–192

Be a word collector, and keep your collection here! Group words any way you like!

Words to Explore

Every spelling lesson has Words to Explore. List them where you think they belong on special pages for . . .

Language...page 184
Social Studies...page 185
Math and Science...page 186
Art and Music...page 187

SIDEWALKS SING Spelling Log • Harcourt Brace School Publishers

The Words to Study pages have a box for each unit in your spelling book. In each box, write the words from that unit that you need to work on more.

Be sure to list the words you missed on the pretests. Put in other words from the unit that you are not sure you can spell correctly.

Unit 1

I'm going to use the study steps on pages 8 and 9 to help me learn these words!

SIDEWALKS SING Spelling Log • Harcourt Brace School Publishers

WORDS TO STUDY

Unit 2

Unit 3

SIDEWALKS SING Spelling Log • Harcourt Brace School Publishers

Here are the pages for the words you need to study in Units 4, 5, and 6.

The words I've listed will be easy to find when I'm ready to study them!

Unit 4

Don't forget to use the study steps on pages 8 and 9 to help you learn these words!

SIDEWALKS SING Spelling Log • Harcourt Brace School Publishers

Integrated Spelling

WORDS TO STUDY

Unit 5

Unit 6

SIDEWALKS SING Spelling Log • Harcourt Brace School Publishers

Integrated Spelling

Words to Explore

Language Words

These pages are for listing Words to Explore. Write words that you think go together in a group. The clues on the sides give you some ideas about ways to group words. Use ideas of your own, too!

Words

Words

SIDEWALKS SING Spelling Log • Harcourt Brace School Publishers

Words
to Explore

If you like, add a clue beside a word to help you remember it. The clue might be a picture, a sentence, or just a word. Here's what I'm going to add to help me remember what a fiesta is.

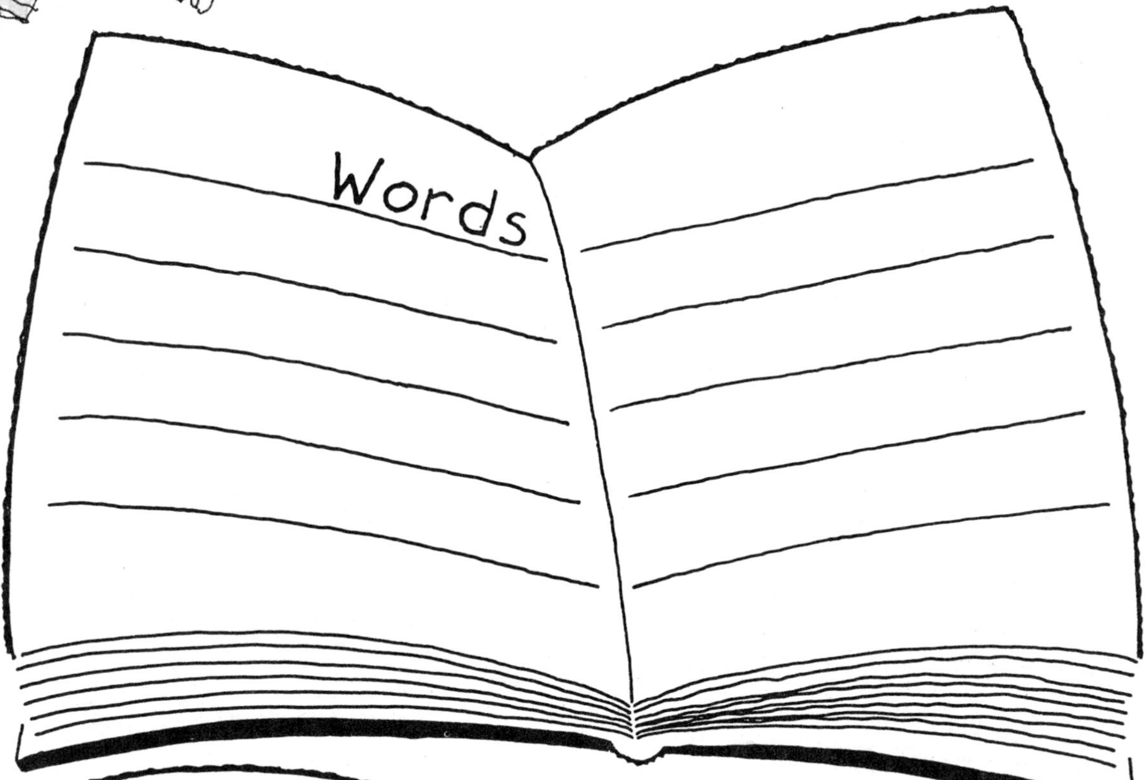

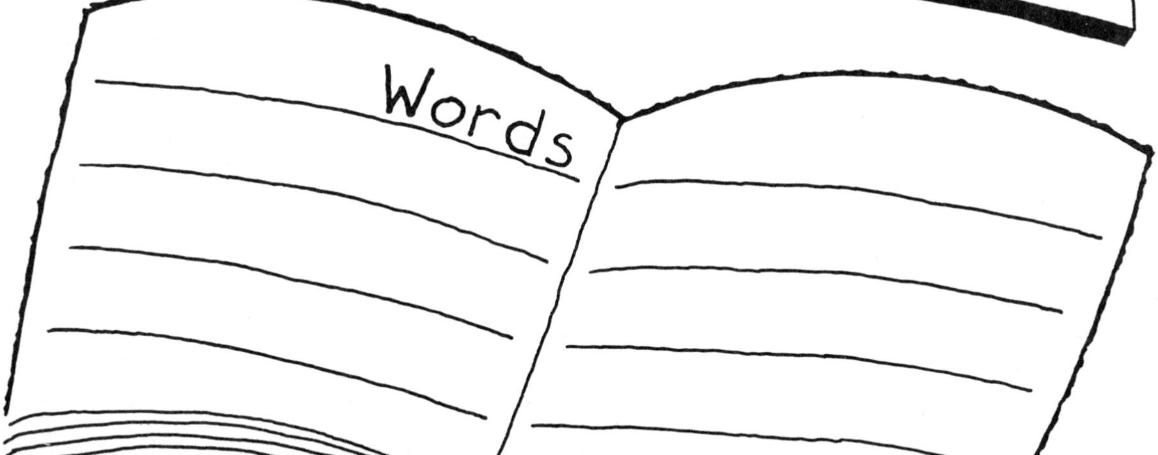

Fiesta

Words

Words

SIDEWALKS SING Spelling Log • Harcourt Brace School Publishers

A family words
money words
Doctor WORDS
Sports words
country words
CITY WORDS

Integrated Spelling

WEATHER words

OCEAN WORDS

ZOO ANIMAL WORDS

UNDER THE GROUND WORDS

Sunny WORDS

STORMY WORDS

Words
to Explore

Math and Science
Words

I'm going to group math
and science words, and write
them on this page.

Words

Words

Words

SIDEWALKS SING Spelling Log • Harcourt Brace School Publishers

Words to Explore

Art and Music Words

This page is for art and music words!

Words

Words

Words

Painting words

Red paint

Yellow paint

LOUD WORDS

WEAVING WORDS

Sewing WORDS

SIDEWALKS SING Spelling Log • Harcourt Brace School Publishers

SIDEWALKS SING Spelling Log • Harcourt Brace School Publishers

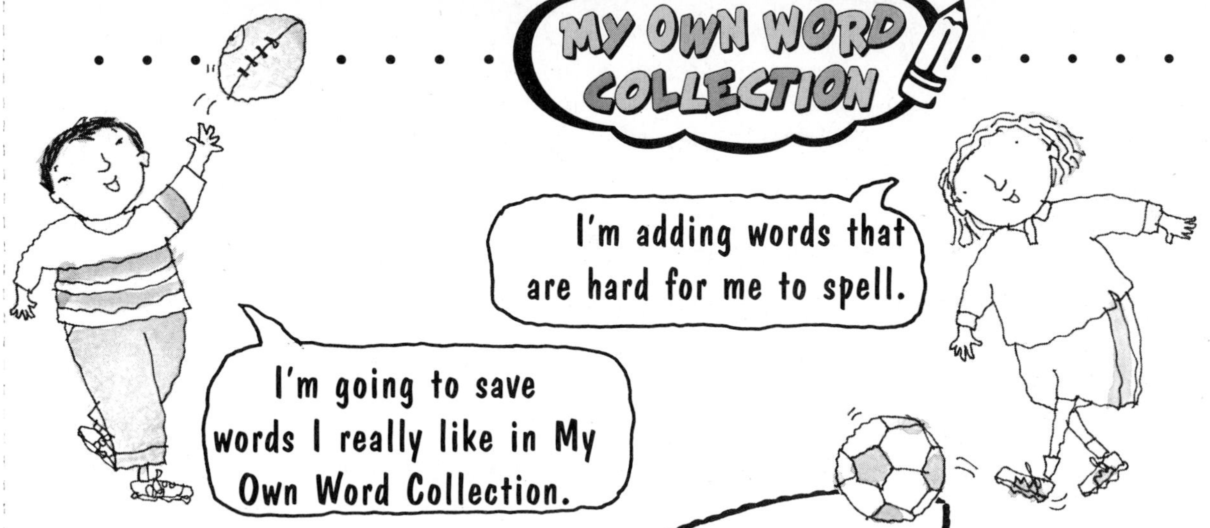

I'm adding words that are hard for me to spell.

I'm going to save words I really like in My Own Word Collection.

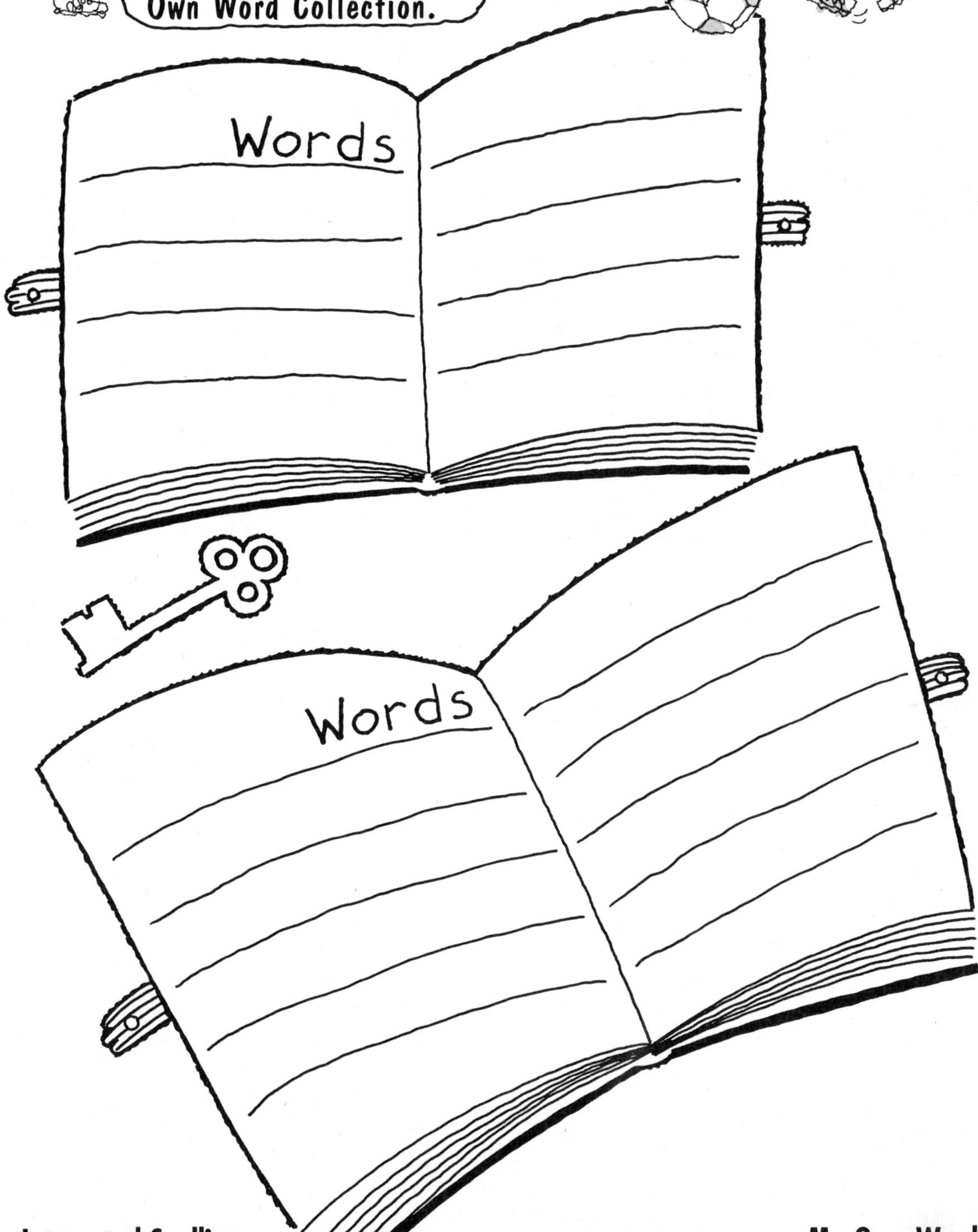

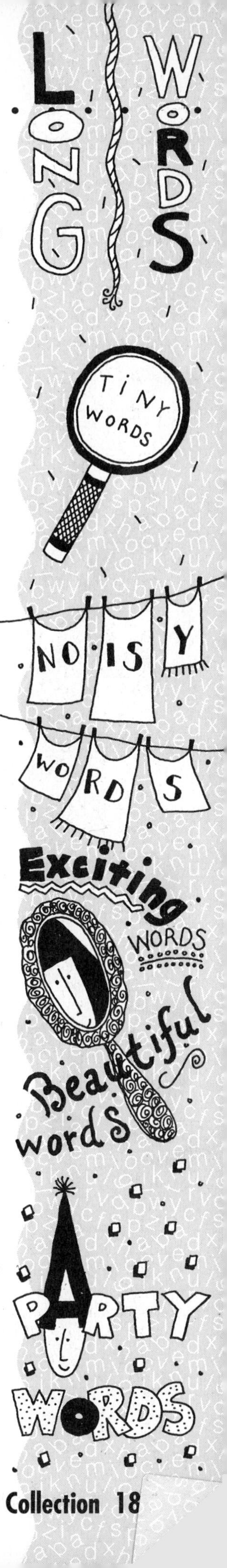

LONG WORDS

TINY WORDS

NOISY WORDS

Exciting WORDS

Beautiful words

PARTY WORDS

Words

Words

Integrated Spelling

NEW
·WORDS·

Co/d
WORDS

FUN
WORDS

words

hard-to-say
WORDS

FOOD
words...

YuKKy
words

MY OWN WORD
COLLECTION

I'm listing the
names of shells in my
word collection!

Words

Words

Integrated Spelling

SIDEWALKS SING Spelling Log • Harcourt Brace School Publishers

MY OWN WORD COLLECTION

I'm writing my favorite new word!

Words

Words

SIDEWALKS SING Spelling Log • Harcourt Brace School Publishers

LONG WORDS

TiNY WORDS

NOISY WORDS

Exciting WORDS

Beautiful words

PARTY WORDS

NEW ·WORDS·

Cold WORDS

FUNNY words

hard-to-say WORDS

FOOD words...

Yukky words

MY OWN WORD COLLECTION

I'm going to group these words when I have time.

Words to Put into Groups Later

Words

SIDEWALKS SING Spelling Log • Harcourt Brace School Publishers

Integrated Spelling